101 CARD GAMES

By David Galt

Publications International, Ltd.

David Galt is a game designer and consultant who has written extensively on games old and new. His articles have appeared in *Games* magazine and *The Playing Card*, and he is also the author of *Card Games for One or Two* and *All-Time Favorite Card Games.* Some of his own game creations are Intense Bridge, Queens, and Molimba.

Illustrator: Jane Sanders
Cover Illustrator: Guy Wolek

Louis Weber, CEO
Publications International, Ltd.
7373 N. Cicero Avenue
Lincolnwood, Illinois 60712

Manufactured in China.

8 7 6 5 4 3 2 1

ISBN: 0-7853-3959-0

Contents

♠ ♦ ♣ ♥

All in the Cards 6

Multi-Player Games 8

Acey-Deucey 8

Auction Pitch 10

Barbu 12

Bezique 15

Rubicon Bezique 18

Chinese Bezique 20

Contract Bridge. 22

Auction Bridge 31

Honeymoon Bridge. . . . 33

Reverse Bridge. 34

Three-Handed Bridge . . 35

Calabrasella 36

Canasta 38

Italian Canasta. 42

Pennies From Heaven . . 44

Samba 45

Three-Handed Cut-Throat. 46

Casino. 47

Royal Casino 51

Concentration 52

Moving Concentration . 54

Coon Can 55

Crazy Eights 58

Double Crazy Eights . . . 60

Cribbage 61

Demon 66

Durock 68

Eleusis 72

Euchre. 75

Fan Tan 79

Gleek. 81

Go Fish 83

Hearts 85

Two-Handed Hearts . . . 89

I Doubt It 91

Kaluki 94

Kings in the Corner. . . . 97

Klaberjass 100

Knaves. 105

Leopard. 106

Michigan. 109

Molimba 112

Nap or Napoleon. 114

Oh Hell! 116

Old Maid 119

Panguingue 120

Pinochle 124
Partnership Pinochle . . 129
Two-Handed Pinochle. 131
Piquet 134
Poker. 138
Draw Poker 143
Stud Poker. 145
Texas Hold 'Em. 146
Anaconda 147
Chicago. 149
Cincinnati 150
Follow the Queen 152
Omaha 153
Pineapple. 154
Razz 155
Seven-Card No Peekie. . 156
Star Wars. 157
Super Hold 'Em 157
President 158
Rummy. 162
Gin Rummy 163
500 Rummy 167
Knock Rummy 169
Oklahoma 170
Schafkopf 174
Sixty-Six 177
Solo. 180
Spades 184
Spite and Malice 187
Twenty-One 191
2-10-Jack. 193
War 196
Whist 198
Whistlet 199

Solitaire Games 202
Accordion 202
Black Hole. 204
Calculation 205
Canfield. 208
Cross Currents. 210
Forty Thieves. 212
Four Corners. 215
Gaps 217
Good Neighbors 219
Grandfather's Clock. . . 220
Klondike 222
Lucky Fours. 225
Miss Milligan 227
Osmosis. 229
Poker Solitaire 231
Propeller 233
Seventeens. 235
The Snake 237
Spider 239
The Sultan of Turkey. . 242
Tut's Tomb 244
Bonus Game 246

Glossary 250

♠ ♦ ♣ ♥ ♠ ♦ ♣ ♥ ♠ ♦ ♣ ♥ ♠ ♦ ♣ ♥ ♠ ♦

All in the Cards

♠ ♦ ♣ ♥

Could you spend an afternoon or evening happily immersed in a card game with good friends? Is a good hand of solitaire one of your favorite pursuits? Well, you're not the first to enjoy this pastime—for the past 600 years, card games have been a great way for people of all ages to have fun!

In *101 Card Games* you'll find a compendium of games to suit every get-together or quiet moment alone. From solitaires to games for a party group, we've assembled card games to suit all tastes and occasions. Some are new; others have a rich, centuries-long history. Some involve nuance and strategy and will take some time to master; others can be picked up in minutes. All are wonderfully entertaining.

In the following pages you'll find instructions for some of the most popular card games of all time. All the games are carefully and clearly explained so that even inexperienced card players can easily learn to play. You will find rules of play, game objectives, suggested number of players, card requirements, and scoring rules. Also included are tips to help you formulate a strategy, as well as variations for modifying games. The rules provided are merely guidelines; once you get the hang of playing, you might just develop your own variations. For beginners, the handy glossary at the back of the book defines important terms and card-table jargon.

Even if you're an "old hand" at cards, you'll find some games you haven't tried, as well as a few new wrinkles in games you thought you knew well. If you're new to card-playing, this is the place to learn the basics of a large variety of games. Whatever your experience, if you're looking to deal out some fun, this book is your best bet.

Acey-Deucey

♠ ♦ ♣ ♥

This card game is a popular wagering game. It's also called Yablon, Between the Sheets, and Red Dog (in casinos).

Number of players: Two or more with one selected as the banker. All others bet against the banker.

Object: To win the bets you place.

The cards: Usually four or five decks, all cards shuffled together, known as a shoe. You may play with fewer or more decks. Aces are high.

To play: You'll need a supply of chips and to set a betting limit. Choose a banker, who is also the dealer. Players each bet. Then banker deals two cards face up. The cards apply to all betting players. If the cards are next to each other in rank (e.g., ♥5, ♦6), all bets are off! Retire those two cards. Players may alter their bet amounts, and dealer turns up two new cards.

If the cards are the same (e.g., two 10s), banker deals up one more card. If it also is the same rank, then banker must pay 11 to 1 on the amounts bet. But if it's any other card, bets again are cancelled, and these three cards are removed.

When the two turned cards have a gap, or spread, in rank (ace high, deuce low), the fun begins. Players who want to may raise their bet up to double their original bet amount. Next, the dealer turns up a third card. If it ranks between the two upcards, the bettors win. But if the third card either matches one of the two upcards or is outside the spread, then the banker wins all bets.

Payoff schedule:

When the card turned falls within a spread of 4–11, banker pays each bettor the amount bet—an even payoff.

When the spread is three (e.g., ♣2-♠6), banker pays twice the bets.

When the spread is two (e.g., ♠7-♦4), banker pays four times the bets.

When the spread is one (e.g., ♥A-♥Q), banker pays six times the bets.

Because the banker has a small edge in this game, the role of banker should rotate among the players.

Tip: The only strategy is deciding when to increase your bet. Whenever the spread is seven or more (e.g., ♠3-♣J), the odds favor you. When the spread is 6 or less, you're bucking the odds if you increase your bet.

♠ ♦ ♣ ♥

♠ ♦ ♣ ♥ ♠ ♦ ♣ ♥ ♠ ♦ ♣ ♥ ♠ ♦ ♣ ♥ ♠ ♦

Auction Pitch

♠ ♦ ♣ ♥

Auction Pitch is a quick game of trumps, filled with strategy and surprise. Also known as Pitch and Setback, it is a descendant of the Mississippi riverboat game Seven Up.

Number of players: Three to five is best, but two to seven may play.

Object: To score points by winning high trump, low trump, jack of trumps, and game.

The cards: A regular deck of 52 cards. Aces are high.

To play: Deal six cards each, in bunches of three. Starting at dealer's left, players each have one chance to pass or bid. A bid is a number one through four, and each bid must be a higher number than any earlier bid.

The high bidder—the pitcher—plays against everybody else. Four possible points can be won in play: high (the highest trump in play), low (the lowest trump in play), jack (the jack of trumps, not always in play), and game (the highest total of cards won in play—aces count 4; kings 3; queens 2; jacks 1; and 10s 10).

The pitcher always begins play by leading (pitching) a card. The suit led becomes trump. Because of this rule, you can silently bid four (the highest bid) simply by pitching a card to indicate your trump lead.

Always follow suit whenever possible. If unable to follow suit, play any card. Each trick is won by the highest trump it contains or, if it contains no trump, by the highest card of the suit led.

Defenders work together to set back the pitcher but keep separate piles of the tricks they've each taken, independently scoring any points earned.

Scoring: If you make your bid, score all the points you won. If you don't make your bid, you lose, or are set back, the number you bid. Defenders score their individually won points. Whoever reaches 7 points wins the game. When two players are near 7, always tally high point first, followed by low, jack, and game.

Tips: A bid of one by the first player is not difficult to make, and will often cause the other players to risk a bid of at least two. An ace is always worth a bid of one, and it will often take two points, since the player with the lowest trump may have to play it. In the unusual case where just one trump is in play, it counts as both high and low. There aren't many cards in play besides the ones you see. In a three-handed game, only 12 other cards are out; in a four-handed game, it's 18. The outcome of most deals is therefore very unpredictable. However, the fewer cards out, the less likely it is that anyone will have the cards needed to set you back. For example, your king of trump will win the high point in a three-handed game nearly 75 percent of the time. For a bid of four, you'll need to have the jack and win it, so your trumps have to be very good to make this bid safely.

♠ ♦ ♣ ♥

♠ ♦ ♣ ♥ ♠ ♦ ♣ ♥ ♠ ♦ ♣ ♥ ♠ ♦ ♣ ♥ ♠ ♦

Barbu

♠ ♦ ♣ ♥

When you play Barbu, a game of French origin, you select from a menu of seven different card games. A complete Barbu session consists of 28 deals.

Number of players: Four, with one chosen as scorekeeper.

Object: To have the highest score at the end of 28 hands.

The cards: Use a regular deck of 52 cards.

To play: Deal 13 cards to each player for each hand. After examining cards, the dealer calls out a "contract" of one of seven games. In five of the games, the goal is basically to avoid winning tricks, while the two remaining games reward you for taking tricks.

These are the five minus-points games.

Nullo (also called No Tricks): Dealer leads any card. The other players in turn from the dealer's left must follow suit, but if a card from that suit is not available, you can discard any card. High card of the led suit wins the trick. The winner then leads for the next trick. There are thirteen tricks in all. At the end of play, each trick counts −2. So if you win no tricks, you score 0 points, the best result possible.

No Last Two Tricks: Same rules as Nullo, but scoring is different. Whoever wins the next to the last trick is penalized −10, and the winner of the final trick receives −20.

No Queens: Same rules as Nullo, except every queen taken scores −6. One custom is to leave the queens taken turned up. Once all four have been played, the hand stops since the score for the deal is already complete.

Hearts (or No Hearts): Same rules as Nullo, but you cannot lead a heart except if that's the only suit you have left in your hand. The object is to take as few ♥s as possible. Every ♥ taken counts −2, with the ♥A counting −6.

Barbu (or No King of Hearts): Same rules as Hearts, except the object is to avoid winning the trick containing the ♥K, which scores −20. Once the ♥K has been taken, play for this hand ceases.

These are the two positive-points games.

Trumps: Dealer declares a trump suit and then leads a card. You must follow suit whenever possible. A few special rules apply. When a trump is led, you must play a higher trump than any played so far, if you can. When a nontrump suit is led and you cannot follow, you must play a trump. You can discard if you have no trumps or if the trick already contains a trump card that you cannot beat. Each trick you take scores +5, resulting in a total of 65 points for this game.

Fan Tan (or Card Dominoes): For the general play of Fan Tan, see the rules in this book under that title. In Fan Tan Barbu-style, the dealer also names the card rank that starts the playoff piles (can be any rank, not just a 7). If declarer says, "Fan Tan 5s," then every suit begins by playing its 5, with players laying off cards in sequence, ascending to king on one side and descending to ace on the other side. The first player to be out

of cards scores +45. The second player to go out scores +20, the third scores +5, and the last player scores −5.

As dealer, you must select a game you have not chosen before until you contract each game only once. Each player may deal seven hands in a row, but it is more interesting for the deal to rotate dealers with each new hand.

Scoring: The scoring chart can get complicated. The scorer not only tallies both + and − scores over 28 deals but also makes sure that each player deals each game only once. After 28 deals, if you have kept score perfectly, the total of all + and − scores will equal 0!

Tips: As dealer, you have the most control because you pick the game and make the first play.

If you have a number of low cards, it usually does not matter which minus-points game you call. Call Trumps when you deal yourself a long suit (at least five or six cards) along with some other high cards.

Bezique

♠ ♦ ♣ ♥

Bezique, the forerunner of Pinochle, was invented in the early 1800s in Sweden. By the 1850s, it was a hit all across Europe, and it soon arrived in America. It's still widely enjoyed in Britain.

Number of players: Two

Object: To score points by melding and by taking tricks containing aces and 10s (brisques).

The cards: Two sets of 32 cards, consisting of aces through 7s, are shuffled together into one 64-card deck. Cards rank—from high to low—A-10-K-Q-J-9-8-7.

To play: Deal eight cards to each player (in groups of three, two, and three), and then turn up a card to designate trumps. Place that card face up and so that it is slightly sticking out from under the draw pile. If the trump upcard is a 7, dealer scores 10 points immediately.

Nondealer starts play by leading any card. At this stage of play, and as long as there remain cards to draw, you are not obliged to follow suit, you may play any of your cards.

The highest trump in a trick wins it, or, if there is no trump card, the highest card of the suit led wins it. When two identical cards contend for the same trick (for example, two ♥10s), the first one played wins the trick.

The winner of each trick scores 10 points for each ace or 10 (brisque) it contains, and may also table one meld. (You may tally the 10 points for a 7 of trumps along with a meld, and if you table the first 7 of trumps you may also trade it for the trump upcard.) Tally all points when you meld as you score them. Tally brisques at the end of the hand.

Both players take a new card from the stock, with the winner of the previous trick drawing first and then leading to the next trick.

Melded cards stay on the table until the stock is used up, but you may still play them on tricks. A card you meld one time can be used again, but only in a different meld and only with a winning trick. For example: ♣Q melds with ♣K in a marriage and can also meld later for 60 points with ♥Q-♦Q-♠Q. But it can't meld with a second ♣K—a completely new pair is needed to score the second marriage.

When only the upcard and one draw card remain, the upcard goes to the trick-loser. Put your remaining melded cards back in your hand, with the winner of the previous trick taking the last draw card and leading to the next trick. In the play of the final eight cards, each player must follow suit and also must win a trick whenever possible. Whoever wins the final trick scores an extra 10 points.

Scoring: The first player to accumulate 1,000 points—or any other agreed-upon sum—wins.

Tips: The play in Bezique has 32 tricks, in which your opponent will try to trump any ace or 10 you lead. Therefore, you should save your 10s to win lower cards when your opponent leads. Meanwhile,

Melds in Bezique:

Trump marriage (K-Q)	40 points
Non-trump marriage (K-Q in same suit)	20 points
Trump flush (A-10-K-Q-J)	250 points
Bezique (♠Q-♦J)	40 points
Double bezique (♠Q-♦J-♠Q-♦J)	500 points
Any four aces	100 points
Any four kings	80 points
Any four queens	60 points
Any four jacks	40 points
7 of trumps (each)	10 points

there's usually a difficult suit for your opponent to win tricks in. Even if you lead low cards of that suit, it may cause discomfort: Players want to hold on to melding cards (aces, kings, queens, the 10 and jack of trumps, and ♠Q and ♦J for a possible 500-point double bezique). Yet each player can hold just eight cards! If you have a big meld near the end of the game—for example, ♠Q-♠Q-♦J-♦J—you may not have time to meld it in two stages to score an extra 40 points. Your opponent may see through that plan and prevent you from winning a second trick and the additional 500 points.

♠ ♦ ♣ ♥ ♠ ♦ ♣ ♥ ♠ ♦ ♣ ♥ ♠ ♦ ♣ ♥ ♠ ♦

Rubicon Bezique

♠ ♦ ♣ ♥

Rubicon Bezique became very popular because of its emphasis on melding.

Number of players: Two

Object: To attain the better score. Each deal is one game. A losing player scoring under 1,000 points is said to be rubiconed.

The cards: Two 64-card Bezique decks (128 cards total).

To play: This game is similar to regular Bezique, but deal nine cards instead of eight. The first melded marriage determines the trump suit. There is no trump until a marriage is declared. If you're dealt a carte blanche (no picture cards), show it and score 50, and score 50 more after each draw until you do get a picture card!

Scoring: New melds include triple bezique (1,500 points), quadruple bezique (4,500 points) and back-door (nontrump A-K-Q-J-10=150 points). A meld can be remade even by replacing a played melded card for a trick! Although the winner of a trick still gathers the two played cards, brisques (aces and tens) are not scored unless they are needed to break a tie or to allow a player to avoid being rubiconed. If one player counts

Dealt this hand, you want to win a trick so that you can exchange the ♥ 7 for the ♥ K (pulled out here for clarity), giving you an immediate 40-point trump marriage (♥ K-♥ Q). You should not play an ace, which would reduce your chance to complete a meld of 4 aces. The ♣ 10 is a possible lead, though it gives opponent the chance to win a brisque. Instead, you could try either ♠ J, but as a card of lower rank, it is a more likely loser.

brisques, both must count them. Last trick counts 50 points. The 7 of trumps is not scored. No declarations are scored after the stock pile is depleted. The player with the highest score at the end of the game adds 500 points. If the loser is rubiconed, the winner receives a 1,000-point bonus instead of 500 as well as 320 credit for brisques, plus all the opponent's points!

♠ ♦ ♣ ♥

♠ ♦ ♣ ♥ ♠ ♦ ♣ ♥ ♠ ♦ ♣ ♥ ♠ ♦ ♣ ♥ ♠ ♦

Chinese Bezique

♠ ♦ ♣ ♥

Chinese Bezique, or Six-Pack Bezique, is fast paced and high scoring; it was Winston Churchill's favorite game.

Number of players: Two

Object: To score a high number of points. Each deal is one game. Loser must reach 3,000 points or be rubiconed.

The cards: Three 64-card Bezique packs (192 cards total).

To play: Players cut to determine dealer, with the choice going to the player with the high card. Cut again if cards are the same rank. It is a disadvantage to be dealer. Deal 12 cards each. It is common to pile up cards played in tricks on the table, where all can see what's been played. Or you may collect them in a neat pile. Brisques and sevens are not scored. There is no trump until the first marriage determines the trump. That trump remains in the next game until that game's first marriage is declared.

Scoring: If dealer lifts 24 cards from the deck when cutting cards at the outset, dealer scores 250 points. If nondealer guesses the correct number of lifted cards,

Chinese Bezique:

Meld scores are as in Rubicon Bezique, with these additional scores:

Four aces of trump	1,000
Four tens of trump	900
Four kings of trump	800
Four queens of trump	600
Four jacks of trump	400

that player scores 150 points. Carte blanche scores 250, and 250 with each succeeding drawn card that is not a face card. Winning the last trick earns 250. The other melds are scored in subsequent winning tricks. The winner of the game receives an additional 1,000 points. If the loser is rubiconed, the winner scores that additional 1,000 points plus the loser's points.

Tip: Remember, you can score again for a meld just by replacing one card. So after melding four kings, if you play one and can replace it later, you score for the entire meld again. In this way you will not only increase your score, but you might also attain the points needed for game.

♠ ♦ ♣ ♥ ♠ ♦ ♣ ♥ ♠ ♦ ♣ ♥ ♠ ♦ ♣ ♥ ♠ ♦

Contract Bridge

♠ ♦ ♣ ♥

Contract Bridge took off as an international rage in the 1930s and is considered today by many to be the ultimate card game. Even those who have been playing for decades still find room to learn.

Number of players: Four, playing as two pairs, with partners facing each other. Tradition refers to the pairs as North-South and East-West.

Object: Following an auction, to score points by taking tricks during the play and to eventually win a rubber of two games.

The cards: Each deal requires a regular pack of 52 cards. Keep a second pack ready for the next hand.

To play: After all the cards have been dealt out, dealer begins the auction (also called the bidding). When the bidding is over, the play of the hand starts. The play comprises 13 tricks in all.

Understanding the bidding: Most games with auctions or bids use a brief and simple procedure. Bridge is special in allowing players to have a creative and complex auction.

In Bridge, players on both sides bid for their side's right to choose the trump suit or to play the hand at

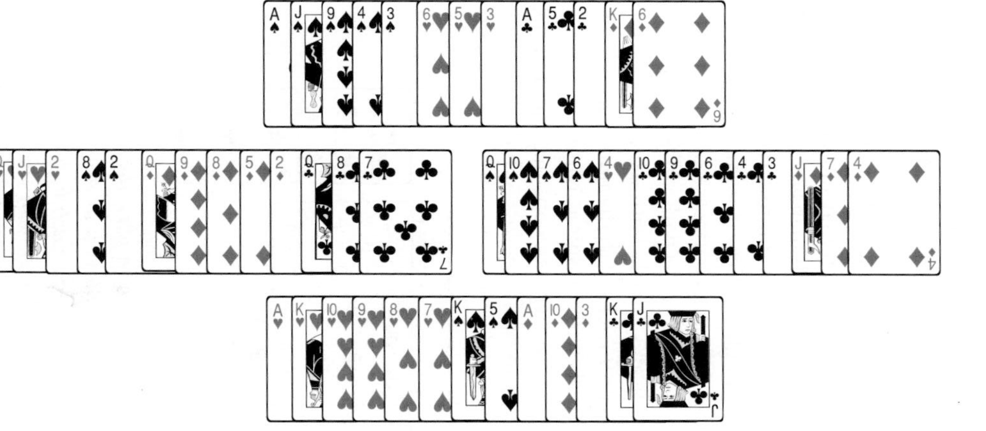

In the diagrammed deal, West deals and passes, and North opens the bidding 1♠. East passes. South bids 2♥. West passes. North bids 3♥ and, after East passes, South bids 6♥. This is a bid to take 12 out of the 13 tricks on the hand, which South expects to happen. The next three players all pass. South, the first to bid ♥s for the winning bidders, becomes declarer at a contract of 6♥.

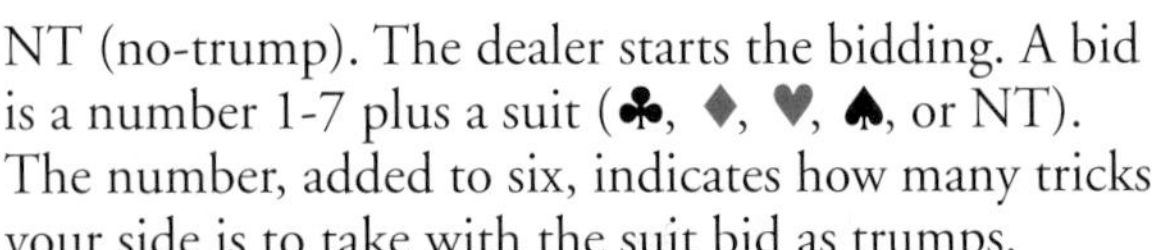

NT (no-trump). The dealer starts the bidding. A bid is a number 1-7 plus a suit (♣, ♦, ♥, ♠, or NT). The number, added to six, indicates how many tricks your side is to take with the suit bid as trumps.

Each time it's your turn, you may bid or pass (make no bid). Simply put, if you can manage to win the bid at a suit in which your side has more cards than the other side has, it will greatly help in winning tricks.

The lowest bid, 1♣, is a contract your side would fulfill by taking at least 7 tricks with clubs as trumps. Similarly, 1♦ indicates 7 tricks with diamonds as trumps; 3♦ means 9 tricks with diamonds as trumps; 3 NT means 9 tricks with no suit as trumps.

The bidding can start with any opening bid. During the auction, players in turn may pass or bid (or in

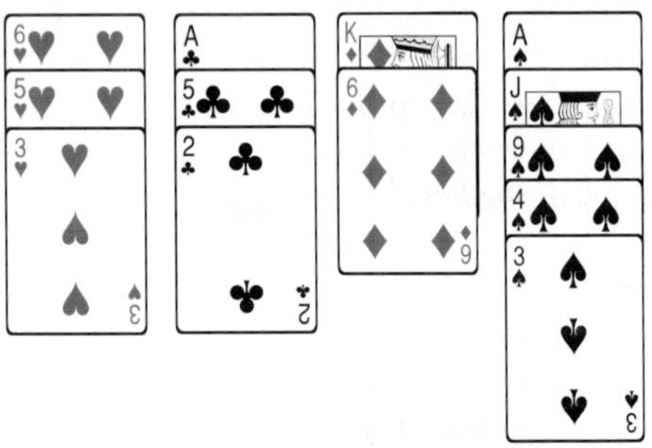

When it is dummy's turn to play, declarer selects the card to be played and plays it or asks dummy to play what the declarer selects. Each hand in playing to a trick must follow with a card of the suit led, but lacking that suit may play any card. Whichever hand wins a trick will lead any card to the next trick.

frequent cases, may double or redouble). Each new bid must be higher than the previous bid. The new bid may be in a higher-ranking suit without increasing the number of tricks: ♣s rank lowest, followed by ♦, ♥, ♠, and NT. (In Bridge, ♥s and ♠s are called majors; ♣s and ♦s are called minors.) Or, if you go to a higher number of tricks, you can bid in any suit or NT.

The auction ends as soon as three players in a row pass. The last bid becomes the final contract. The last bidder is called the declarer. By the way, don't let any other player see your cards during the auction.

Double and redouble: If your opponent has made the most recent bid, at your turn you may double (just say the word "double"). This means you double the stakes, i.e., if you make your contract, you win double the number of points—your risk is also correspondingly greater. Either opponent can then redouble. Three passes end every auction, so it's quite possible for the final contract to be doubled or redoubled, increasing the score.

The play of the hand: In the deal shown (on p. 23), West, the player at declarer's left, will choose the card to lead to the first trick. This is called the opening lead. Once the opening lead is made, the dummy hand, (declarer's partner, here North), is placed on the table. North rearranges it to show trumps (♥s) on the left.

West begins by lending the ♦5. Playing low from dummy, South wins East's ♦J with the ♦A. At tricks two and three, South cashes (takes short tricks) his ♥A and ♥K, and discovers that the defense will win a trick with the ♥Q. That's okay, as South will win every other trick. South continues at the fourth trick

♠ ♦ ♣ ♥ ♠ ♦ ♣ ♥ ♠ ♦ ♣ ♥ ♠ ♦ ♣ ♥ ♠ ♦

Bridge Scoring:

Contract level	minors (♣ or ♦)	majors (♥ or ♠)	NT
1	20	30	40
2	40	60	70
3	60	90	100
4	80	120	130
5	100	150	160
6	120	180	190
7	140	210	220

by leading the ♦3 to dummy's ♦K, and then comes back to hand by leading ♠3 to the ♠K. South next leads the ♦10, West puts on the ♦Q, but South trumps it in dummy with dummy's remaining trump. Except for West's high ♥, South will win all the tricks and the contract succeeds.

Scoring: After the tricks have been played, it is clear whether the declarer made the contract or, instead, went down. If the contract is made, the declaring side scores according to the table above. If you make a contract of 6, it's called a small slam; a grand slam is a made contract of 7 bids. Both slams receive bonuses. If you win six or seven tricks but did not bid that number, you are not credited with a slam.

If the contract goes down, the other side scores points for undertricks, that is, the number of tricks the declaring side falls short of the contract (see opposite).

Scoring for undertricks:

"Down" means number of tricks short of the contract.

	Not vulnerable	Doubled	Redoubled
Down 1	50	100	200
Down 2	100	300	600
Down 3	150	500	1000
Down 4	200	800	1600
Down 5	250	1100	2200
Down 6	300	1400	2800

	Vulnerable	Doubled	Redoubled
Down 1	100	200	400
Down 2	200	500	1,000
Down 3	300	800	1,600
Down 4	400	1100	2,200
Down 5	500	1400	2,800
Down 6	600	1700	3,400

Rubber Bridge scoring: When one side has scored two games, it wins the rubber. A game means 100 points in tricks bid for (and won) according to the scoring table at left. It's quite possible to bid and make game on a single deal: For example, 3 NT scores 100 points, and successful contracts of 4♥, 4♠, 5♣, and

Scoring for bonuses:

Rubber bonus: 500 (2 games to 1), or 700 (2 games to 0)

Slam bonuses: Small slam: 500 not vulnerable, 750 vulnerable

Grand slam: 1,000 not vulnerable, 1,500 vulnerable

Bonus for making doubled contract: 50

Bonus for making redoubled contract: 100

Honors: All four aces in one hand, at a NT contract: 150

Top 5 trumps all in one hand: 150

4 of 5 top trumps all in one hand: 100

Overtricks: Undoubled (each): ♣ or ♦, 20; ♥, ♠ or NT, 30

Doubled (each): not vulnerable, 100, vulnerable 200

Redoubled (each): not vulnerable, 200, vulnerable 400

5♦ also count at least 100 points. Alternatively, you can earn game in a series of deals whose final contracts end at a lower bidding level; these are called part-scores or partials. For example, you might bid and make 2♦ on one hand (40 points), and on the next hand you might bid and make 2♥ (60 points). The two added together equal 100 points, enough for game.

A side that has scored one game is vulnerable, so

Useful Bridge Terms

Auction: bidding for number of tricks to be taken in the game

Contract: number of tricks declarer must take to satisfy his or her bid

Declarer: winner of the auction, the player who tries to make the contract

Dummy: declarer's partner; the dummy hand is laid face up on the table

Double: in the auction a bid to double the score or the penalties if a contract is made or set

Major: a heart or spade card

Minor: a diamond or club card

Response: your call in the auction when your partner has opened the bidding

Raise: a bid in a suit that partner has already bid

Overcall: a bid made after opponents have opened the bidding

Set: to defeat a contract

Undertricks: number of tricks the declaring side falls short of the contract

Table: the dummy

Rubber: two games

Ruff: to trump

Singleton: just one card of a suit

Void: no cards in a suit

Vulnerable: a side that has won a game in a rubber

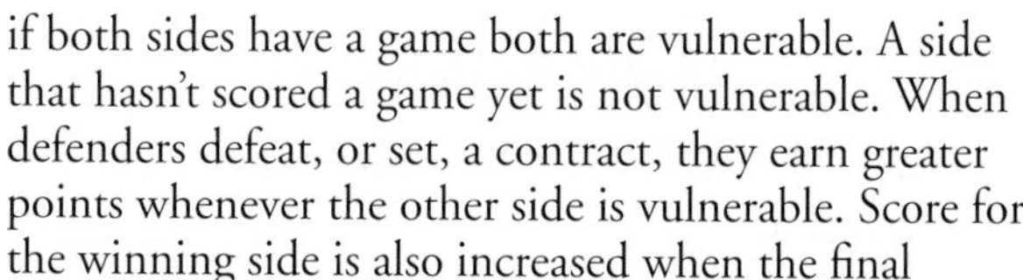

if both sides have a game both are vulnerable. A side that hasn't scored a game yet is not vulnerable. When defenders defeat, or set, a contract, they earn greater points whenever the other side is vulnerable. Score for the winning side is also increased when the final contract is doubled or redoubled. Note: Extra tricks (overtricks) made at any contract do not count toward game.

Bridge Score:

N-S	E-W
700	100
750	30
120	40
180	

Scoring above and below the line: Both sides usually keep score, either on a preprinted Bridge score pad, or else just by drawing lines in a cross.

Points toward game go below the line, while all other points, including bonuses and overtricks, score above the line. In the diagram, E-W bid 1NT and made 2NT, scoring 40 below the line and 30 above for the overtrick. Then N-S bid 4♥ and made 120. To show that a game was won, an additional line was added under that score. E-W's 40 part-score, by the way, is wiped out; E-W earn the points but both sides start fresh earning 100 trick points toward the next game. N-S then bid 3♦ but went down one vulnerable, earning E-W 100 above the line. Finally, N-S bid and made 6♥ (in the hand shown), scoring 180 below the line in trick score, 750 above the line for vulnerable small slam bonus, and 700 more points above the line for winning a rubber two games to none. In this instance, the total rubber score is N-S 1,750, E-W 170.

Tips and strategy: Remembering the cards played is one key to improving your play. This will occur over time. As a start, make sure to notice and remember the first time someone doesn't follow to a trick. It also helps to develop an ease with the number 13! That's the number of cards in a suit, the number or cards each player is dealt, and the number of tricks in the play.

More books have been written on Bridge than on any other card game, so go to the library or bookstore and explore the bidding styles and tips for good card-play.

♠ ♦ ♣ ♥

Auction Bridge

♠ ♦ ♣ ♥

Auction Bridge had its heyday from about 1900 to 1930, before yielding to Contract Bridge.

Number of players: Four

Object: To score points. In Auction Bridge, if you take enough tricks, you score game and slam bonuses without regard to how high the bidding ended.

The cards: A regular pack of 52 cards.

To play: The auction, procedure of play, and rules of play are already described in Contract Bridge.

Scoring: Auction Bridge underwent several scoring changes, and this is the final version. A rubber ends

when one side scores two games. Game is 30 points in trick-score: ♣, ♦, ♥, ♠, and NT score 6, 7, 8, 9, and 10 points per trick, scored below the line. When one side reaches 30, both sides start anew on the next game. Winning the rubber (two games) earns a 250-point bonus.

Winning 12 of 13 tricks earns a 50-point small slam bonus, and winning all 13 tricks (a grand slam) receives a 100-point reward. Making doubled or redoubled contracts doubles or redoubles the trick-score. Overtricks (extra tricks made) at a doubled contract count 50 each, and redoubled overtricks are 100 each. Failing to make a contract costs 50 per trick undoubled, 100 doubled, and 200 redoubled. Bonuses are given to hands that contain any of the following: 3 of top 5 honors (A, K, Q, J, and 10 of trump) or 3 aces at NT (may be divided between hands), 30 points; 4 honors or 4 aces at NT (divided), 40 points; 5 trump honors divided, 50 points; 4 trump honors in one hand, 80 points; 4 trump honors in one hand, with 5th in partner's hand, 100 points; 4 aces in one hand (at NT), 100 points; 5 honors in one hand, 150 points.

Tips: The bidding in Auction is less sophisticated than in Contract Bridge, since the main idea is to buy the contract at a low level. But you might not have found the best suit for your side.

Look to take as many tricks as you can, since it is possible to win a game or slam on every hand.

Honeymoon Bridge

♠ ♦ ♣ ♥

This is one of the most popular two-player Bridge variants.

Number of Players: Two

To play: This is a great game for honeymooners and other couples. Players sit next to (not opposite) each other. Dealer deals out four hands, including a dummy hand for each player. Deal each dummy hand as follows: First, deal out two rows of three cards face down. Then place one card face up on top of each face-down card. Deal the last card face up next to the rows.

Bid as in normal Bridge, except that a single pass ends the auction. The play goes this way, with each player controlling the cards played from the partner/dummy hand across the table: The hand at declarer's left makes the opening lead. Players select the cards played only from among the exposed cards in their dummy hands. After the trick is finished, turn up any uncovered card in their dummy. Any newly revealed card may now be played.

♠ ♦ ♣ ♥

Reverse Bridge

♠ ♦ ♣ ♥

This four-handed game turns all the rules upside-down!

To play: Rules and play are as in regular Bridge, but the object is entirely the opposite: You try to force opponents to take the tricks for the bid you make. So, if your side wins a final contract of 4♠, your job is to get your opponents to take at least 10 of 13 tricks with ♠ as trumps. You get the score for any contract you force the opponents to make!

Strategy: Instead of saving the high cards your side holds to play on different tricks, as in regular Bridge, you'll play as high a card as you can that you think will still lose a trick. When your side does take a trick, try to put high cards on it from both hands so that you can save your losing cards to help you later in the hand!

♠ ♦ ♣ ♥

♠ ♦ ♣ ♥ ♠ ♦ ♣ ♥ ♠ ♦ ♣ ♥ ♠ ♦ ♣ ♥ ♠ ♦

Three-Handed Bridge

♠ ♦ ♣ ♥

Waiting for a fourth player to show up, lots of folks have sought ways for only three players to enjoy Bridge. Though no method comes close to the real thing, here's one way to have some fun.

Number of players: Three

To play: Deal out four hands, with the fourth hand (which will become a dummy) left on the table opposite the dealer with four cards turned up. Players will bid for the right to become declarer opposite the dummy on the table, and play out the contract against the two other players, who will defend.

Before bidding, each player including dealer looks at three of the face-down cards from the dummy, and then returns them face down, but sorted into suits.

Dealer begins the bidding, and the final contract is agreed to after two passes. Shift places, if needed, to bring declarer opposite the dummy hand.

After the opening lead, turn up the nine face-down dummy cards to let declarer see the entire dummy before planning a line of play.

Scoring: The scoring is the same as in Contract Bridge, but it can get a little complicated keeping

track of three scores. A contract may be doubled and redoubled, but that applies to the scores of only the two players involved. The third scores for an undoubled contract.

♠ ♦ ♣ ♥

Calabrasella

♠ ♦ ♣ ♥

This old Italian trick-taking game is lots of fun but takes some getting used to: 3s are high in every suit!

Number of players: Three

Object: To score as many as possible of the 35 points available by trick-taking.

The cards: An Italian deck, or if you don't have one handy, a 40-card deck made by discarding all 8s, 9s, and 10s from a standard pack.

To play: Deal 12 cards to each player, four at a time, and also four in the center of the table as a widow (these should not be the last four). Starting with player at dealer's left, each player says "pass" or "play." If all pass, throw the hands in; the deal passes to the left. Whoever says "play" battles alone against the other two, who now unite as a team.

The lone player discards up to four cards from his or her hand and turns up the four widow cards. The player then takes from the widow the same number of cards that he or she discarded. The discards and the unused widow cards are set aside; they will go to the side that wins the last trick of play. In each suit the 3 is highest, followed by 2, A, K, Q, J, 7, 6, 5, 4. There's never any trump suit.

Player to dealer's left makes the first lead, and the others follow suit if possible. The winner of each trick leads to the next, until all 12 have been played. One opponent keeps the tricks for both. The winner of the final trick also wins the widow and discards. Each side then adds up the points taken.

Scoring: Each suit has 8 points. Five cards—3s, 2s, Ks, Qs, and Js—count 1 point each, while aces count 3. In addition, last trick earns a 3-point bonus, making a total of 35 points for each deal. Whichever side scores more points wins the difference in points between the two scores. Thus, if player scores 21 to opponents' 14, player wins 7 from each opponent.

Canasta

♠ ♦ ♣ ♥

Canasta, the Spanish word for basket, evolved in Uruguay and spread across Latin America in the 1940s. In 1950, the game spread like wildfire across the United States.

Number of players: Four, in partnerships seated across the table.

Object: To score points by melding, with the goal of scoring a canasta and then going out.

The cards: Two regular packs of 52 cards plus their four jokers are used. Jokers and deuces are wild.

Melding: Melds must consist of at least three cards, all of the same rank. All melds are placed face up on the table, and partners build up their melds together to form canastas, seven-card bonus melds. All jokers and deuces are wild and can be used in melds as any desired rank except 3s. A canasta must consist of at least four natural cards but may contain any number of wild cards.

The treys: Red 3s are bonus cards worth 100 points each, but they are not used in play. You should lay down a red 3 as soon as you can. If your side scores all four red 3s, the bonus for them doubles to 800 points.

Black 3s are used in play, but are meldable only when going out. Otherwise, they function as stopper cards (see "Freezing the pack").

To play: Deal 11 cards to each player, one at a time, then turning over an upcard that starts a discard pile called the pack. The remainder of the cards form the

stock. Note: If the upcard is a wild card or a red 3, turn another card up on top of it, and see "Freezing the pack."

The player at dealer's left goes first, with play passing in clockwise rotation until the hand is over. At your turn, even on the first round of play, you may take the pack with an appropriate hand of cards (see "Taking the pack"), but your usual turn consists of drawing one card and then discarding one card on top of the pack.

Taking the pack: You are allowed to take the pack—the entire current pile of discards—as long as you can meld the top discard and meet the following conditions. If your side hasn't melded yet, you'll need two natural (not wild) cards to meld with the upcard, and you must meet the minimum meld required for your side (without using any other cards in the pack). If your side has melded already, then one natural card with one wild card will do, and you may even take the pack if your opponent's discard can go into one of your melds.

Also, once your side has met its initial meld, you may use the pack to form new melds or add to your melds to form canastas, as you wish. Any cards you don't meld become part of your hand.

Once a meld is on the table, either partner may play off it. When a meld contains seven or more cards, it becomes a canasta. It is squared into a pile and a red card is placed on top if it consists of all natural cards (a natural canasta). A black card is placed on top if it contains any wild cards (a mixed canasta). If any wild cards are later added to a red canasta, it becomes a black canasta, and its value changes accordingly.

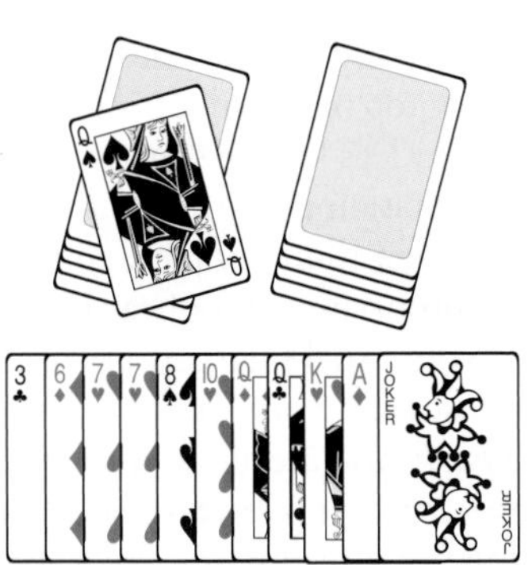

You don't have to take the pack to make an initial meld, but it gives you more cards to play with. Wait until there are enough cards (around 10 to 12) in the pack to take it, so you will have more cards in your hand. In this case, taking the upcard gives you melds worth 90 points: ♦ Q-♣ Q-♠ Q and ♥ 7-♥ 7-joker.

Freezing the pack: Freezing the pack makes it difficult for any player to take the pack. To freeze the pack, discard a wild card sideways across the discards. The next player can't take the pack as long as the wild card remains. To pick up a frozen pack, you'll need a natural pair in your hand to go with top discard. This rule applies to all players, regardless of who froze the pack initially.

A black 3 freezes the pack momentarily, except in the unlikely event that a player with two black 3s can go out while taking the pack. That would require using every card taken in the pack. (Note: Wild cards may not meld with black 3s.)

When a player discards one card face up on the pack, the turn is complete.

Initial melds:

The first player to meld for a side must table at least 50 points of meld. All cards have point values for melding.

Joker	50 points
Deuce	20 points
Ace	20 points
King through 8	10 points
7 through 4	5 points
Black 3s	5 points

To calculate the value of a meld, simply add up the value of the cards it contains. Note that a three-card (or longer) meld must have at least two natural cards. The initial melding requirement increases along the way as detailed in the table below:

Score at the beginning of new deal	*Minimum initial meld*
Less than 0	15 points
0–1495	50 points
1500–2995	90 points
3000 or more	120 points

Going out: You go out (sometimes called going rummy) if you meld all the cards in your hand. However, in order to go out, your side has to have at least

one canasta, and in most games you need one card left over to discard. Play ceases at this point, and the score for the hand is tallied. Before going out, you are allowed to ask your partner "May I go out?" but you must abide by the answer. Should no one go rummy, the hand ends when the stock is gone and the pack can't be taken.

Scoring: Total the value of all melded cards and add bonuses for going rummy (100), natural canastas (500), mixed canastas (300), and red 3s (100 each, but 800 for all four). Subtract the total of cards left in each player's hand (red 3s count −200 points), and tally each team's score. Game is 5,000 points.

Tip: When taking the pack, don't meld everything in it immediately. It is wise to keep some cards so that you'll have natural pairs to take a frozen pack.

♠ ♦ ♣ ♥

Italian Canasta

♠ ♦ ♣ ♥

Can't get enough Canasta? Try this exciting, high-scoring version!

Number of players: Four
Object: To score a game of 12,000 points.
The cards: Three decks with their six jokers, 162 cards in all.

Melding requirements

The initial melds must be made without wild cards. The requirements are as follows:

Score	*Minimum initial meld*
Over 5,000	160 points
7,500–9,995	180 points
Over 10,000	200 points

To play: Deal 15 cards, but don't turn up the top card until players have all discarded red 3s. Then, according to the top card's value, add an additional pack of cards to the discard pile. Each player takes a number of cards equal to the rank of the turned card (J=11, Q=12, K=13; A, 2, or joker=20; all others face value). At each turn, draw two cards and discard one.

You may make a meld of just deuces, but may not use a deuce elsewhere until you complete a deuce canasta (e.g., ♠2-♥2-♥2-♣2-♦2-♥2-♣2). Wild card canastas don't count toward going out.

Scoring: There is a 300-point bonus for going out. Red 3s count as follows: up to three, 100 each; four or more, 200 each. Seven deuces counts 3,000, and a mixed wild canasta 2,000, but wild card bonuses only count if your side goes out, otherwise they're card value. Five pure canastas receive 2,000 bonus; five canastas including one mixed 1,000; any ten canastas, 2,000.

♠ ♦ ♣ ♥ ♠ ♦ ♣ ♥ ♠ ♦ ♣ ♥ ♠ ♦ ♣ ♥ ♠ ♦

Pennies From Heaven

♠ ♦ ♣ ♥

Here's a game in the Canasta family with lots of action. Be sure to have plenty of table space!

Number of Players: Six, in two teams of three.

Object: To score a game of 20,000 points. To go out on each deal you'll need one 7s canasta, one wild canasta, one natural, and one mixed.

The cards: Four decks, with eight jokers (216 cards).

To play: Deal 13 cards to each player. Then deal a face-down reserve packet of 11 cards each player may add to their hand after completing a canasta. Draw two cards at each turn and discard one. Canastas of any sort are limited to seven cards. Sevens may not be discarded until each side has a 7s canasta. You may not go out with a 7 as a discard.

Scoring: A canasta of 7s counts 1,500. A wild card canasta counts 1,000. A wild card on top of the pack freezes it. Red 3s count 100 each, and all 8 count 1,000. Your red 3s will be scored against you if your side does not complete a 7s canasta.

♠ ♦ ♣ ♥

♠ ♦ ♣ ♥ ♠ ♦ ♣ ♥ ♠ ♦ ♣ ♥ ♠ ♦ ♣ ♥ ♠ ♦

♠ ♦ ♣ ♥

This is an exciting derivative of Canasta, with sequential suit melds.

Number of players: Four

Object: To score a game of 10,000 points.

The cards: Three decks plus six jokers, (162 cards).

To play: The game is similar to Canasta, but with the following alterations: Deal 15 cards to each player. Players draw two cards and discard one at each turn. A 3,000 to 6,995 score requires a 120-point initial meld; 7,000 and over requires 150. Mixed canastas can have two wild cards maximum. An upcard cannot be taken to add to a canasta, but cards from your hand can be added to a canasta. Score is calculated for each side, but the winning side scores only the difference in scores.

Scoring: There is a 200-point bonus for going out. A samba, an in-suit sequence of seven with no wild cards (i.e., ♦6-7-8-9-10-J-Q), counts 1,500 points. Turn the samba cards over when completed. You need two canastas, two sambas, or one of each to go out and to get credit for your red 3s. Add a 1,000-point bonus if you have all the red 3s.

Tip: The lowest possible card in a samba is a 4, and every samba includes 8-9-10 of a suit, so it is hard to complete two sambas in the same suit.

♠ ♦ ♣ ♥

♠ ♦ ♣ ♥ ♠ ♦ ♣ ♥ ♠ ♦ ♣ ♥ ♠ ♦ ♣ ♥ ♠ ♦

Three-Handed Cut-Throat

♠ ♦ ♣ ♥

This Canasta variation's not nearly as vicious as its title implies, but you will find it truly competitive fun!

Number of players: Three
Object: To reach 7,500 points.
The cards: Two decks plus four jokers
To play: This Canasta variation has these adjustments: Deal 11 cards. After play starts, draw two cards every turn but discard one. Whoever first takes the pack plays against the two others for that hand only. After an initial meld the two become melding partners for the rest of the hand. Partners must still meet their current initial meld requirement.

Scoring: Red 3s are scored for each. You must meld to score positive points for red 3s; otherwise they count as negative points. Partners count their melding and penalty points together, and each scores that amount.

Tips: Usually in Canasta an advantage swings to whichever side takes the pack first. In this game, whoever takes it first wants to get an ample pack of discards, because the other two play combined, with twice as many cards.

♠ ♦ ♣ ♥

Casino

♠ ♦ ♣ ♥

As far back as 1797, Casino was described in books on card games. Though the game has quite a few details, it's easy to learn and fun to play, with lots of suspense and surprise.

Number of players: Two
Object: To score points by taking cards.
The cards: A regular pack of 52 cards is used.
To play: Deal four cards to each player and four cards face up on the table. Dealer keeps the rest of the pack handy. Nondealer plays a card first; players then alternate until the round is over. You can combine the card you play with cards on the table in many possible ways.

Matching: If your card matches by rank a card on the table, you can take the pair immediately. Place the two cards face down in front of you.

Face cards can be taken only with other face cards and only in pairs—if two queens are on the table and you hold another queen, you can take only one of the queens. However, if three matching face cards are on the table and you hold the fourth, you can take all four.

Combining: If your card equals the combined sum of two or more cards on the table, you can take those cards immediately.

Building: If at least one free card on the table plus

the card you play totals the number of a card in your hand, announce this build number and pile up the build to take later. For example, if there is a 6 on the table and you have a 3 and a 9 in your hand, you could play the 3 onto the 6 and say "Building 9s." On your next turn, if opponent hasn't taken it, you can take the build with your 9.

Opponent can change the value of a build by playing another card. In this case, opponent can play an ace on the build and say "Building 10s." This tells you he or she has a 10 with which to take the build.

But if your 9-build is still there and if you have two 9s in your hand, on your next turn you can put one of them on top of the build and say "Still building 9s," intending to take the build with your remaining 9. This creates a double build. Players can't change the value of a double build.

With this Casino hand, you can take the ♦9 with your ♥9 and take the ♥5 and ♠5 with your ♠10.

Scoring:

Players count their cards and note the cards with extra value. Each deal contains 11 points:

♦10 (Big Casino)	2 points
♠2 (Little Casino)	1 point
♠A, ♣A, ♥A, ♦A	1 point each
Majority of spades (7 or more)	1 point

Majority of cards (27 or more) 3 points (If tied at 26 cards, neither player wins these points.)

Once you have made a build, on your next turn you must either take the build, add to the build, or make a new build. Leaving a build untaken runs the risk that opponent will take it, but you may leave a build behind as long as you can add cards to it or make another play.

Nothing prevents you from taking opponent's build; you can do so if you have the right card. On the other hand, nothing prevents your opponent from taking your build!

Trailing: You may also play a card by trailing it—placing it on the table without building it onto another card. You can't do this if you have made a build that's still on the table. You must trail a card if you can't do anything else on your turn. For strategic reasons, a player might want to trail a card onto the table even though it matches the rank of one already there.

After the first round of four cards, dealer deals another round of four cards each and nondealer again plays first. Continue dealing four-card rounds until the pack is depleted, with dealer announcing "last" on the last round. Whoever makes the last take of the last round gets any cards left on the table.

Play to 21 points or to any other agreed number.

Tips: Keeping track of what's been played—particularly the spades and points you've taken in—is critical.

Until it's been played, a certain amount of tension revolves around the ♦ 10, Big Casino. As nondealer, if you have the ♦ 10, you risk losing it if you can't take it in. (Dealer will probably save any 10 as the final card of the round.) Beware of building 10s when your own 10 is not the ♦ 10.

If you are dealt any of the four aces or the ♠ 2, your best chance of taking them in is through building. Test your opponent's hand with a double build. Suppose you're holding an ace, a 3, and a 6, and on the table are a 3 and a 5. You'd really like to take the ace for the point. First you play the 3 on the 3, saying "Building 6s." If opponent doesn't take it, on your next play you place your ace on the 5 to make a double build of 6s—subsequently picking up the lot with your 6.

You can often rack up more points by concentrating on winning cards and spades rather than on the Big Casino and Little Casino.

As dealer, if you are dealt a face card on the last round, you are virtually guaranteed to get last card, since you play last.

♠ ♦ ♣ ♥

♠ ♦ ♣ ♥ ♠ ♦ ♣ ♥ ♠ ♦ ♣ ♥ ♠ ♦ ♣ ♥ ♠ ♦

Royal Casino

♠ ♦ ♣ ♥

Here's a new twist on Casino that adds further strategy to an excellent old game.

To play: Play as regular Casino, with face cards having extra numerical values: Jacks are 11, queens 12, kings 13, aces 1 or 14. A queen, for example, can take an 8 and a 4. Aces on the table count 1, but an ace you play counts as 1 or 14, as you wish. So, an ace and a king on the table can be captured with an ace from your hand, since 1 + 13 = 14.

Tips: In Royal Casino it's tempting to hold on to aces longer, because there's the chance to make or build 14. Just when you decide to play an ace will vary, depending on the cards already played and the other cards in your hand.

Picture cards no longer are taken only in pairs. So, dealer's "automatic" capture of last cards in regular Casino when dealer has at least one face card disappears. A face card at the end of a Royal Casino hand may indeed be an odd card. Or, even when opponent and you each hold a jack, for example, opponent can use it as an 11 and remove it from play.

♠ ♦ ♣ ♥

Concentration

♠ ♦ ♣ ♥

Concentration is often one of the first card games a child learns. In fact, don't be surprised if the youngest participants outplay their elders!

Number of players: Two and up

Object: To gather in the most cards by matching them in pairs.

The cards: A regular pack of 52 cards is used.

To play: You'll need a large surface area. Deal the whole deck out, card by card, face down. It doesn't matter if the cards are in neat rows and columns or in a haphazard arrangement.

A turn of play consists of turning over one card, then another. All players see the turned-up cards. If

These two cards don't match, but remember where they are for later play!

these cards match in rank, remove them from the layout and keep them. Go again.

If the two cards turned aren't the same rank, your turn ends. Return the cards to their places, face down. Try to remember the turned-up cards so that you can match them later.

Scoring: When the cards have all been taken, count them. High scorer after three games wins.

Tips: You can get the feel for this game very quickly. The key to it is visual and spatial recall. If you're not sure which card to turn over, you should always go with your instincts. You'll probably be right more times than not.

Variations: At each turn, you may turn over a third card whenever the first two do not match. If still no pair is produced, return them all to their places. (When down to the final six cards, only two cards may be turned.)

Moving Concentration

♠ ♦ ♣ ♥

Here's the ultimate Concentration challenge. This one's a real memory workout!

To play: Lay out the cards as in Concentration. Now here's the tricky part: When you turn up a pair that doesn't match, you can return the cards to new spots in the layout! The new wrinkle lets you add a little strategy to your Concentration play. If you think you know where the match is to one of the cards you've turned up in a mismatched pair, be sure to note very carefully where you put that card down. Pay attention to whether one of your opponents has a habit of placing cards they think they can match later in a certain spot in the layout.

A bit of strategy might help you in Moving Concentration, but the real key to this game is memory, memory, memory!

♠ ♦ ♣ ♥

Coon Can

♠ ♦ ♣ ♥

A game that appears to have originated down South, Coon Can's name comes from the Spanish ¿con quién? (meaning "with whom?").

Number of players: Two

Object: To go coon can, that is to meld all your cards, plus an extra card you pick from the draw or discard pile.

The cards: A 40-card pack (akin to a Spanish pack), with all 10s, 9s, and 8s removed, is used. This leaves the jack and 7 in sequence. Aces are low.

Melding: Melds in Coon Can must have at least three cards and are left on the table. You may meld cards in long spreads (suit sequences) or short spreads (same rank).

To play: Deal ten cards each and leave the rest face down as a draw pile. Nondealer begins by plucking (turning up) and showing the top card from stock. You cannot add a plucked card to your hand, so if this card is not used in a meld, it must be discarded. Each player in turn then must either take the top discard and meld it or turn up the top card from stock and meld or discard it. If the player takes and melds a discard, that player must discard a card.

During one turn, you may hit your own spreads with any number of cards, but when you hit your

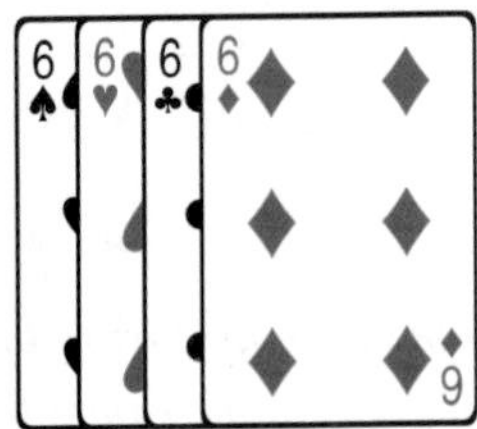

Short spreads

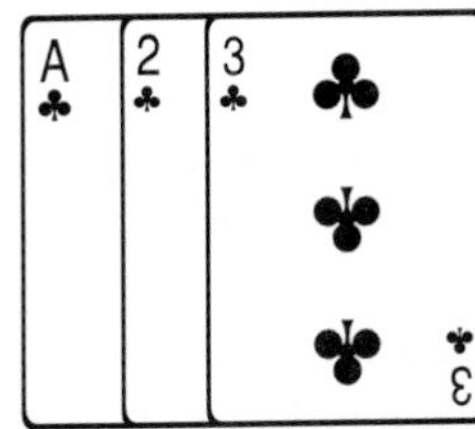

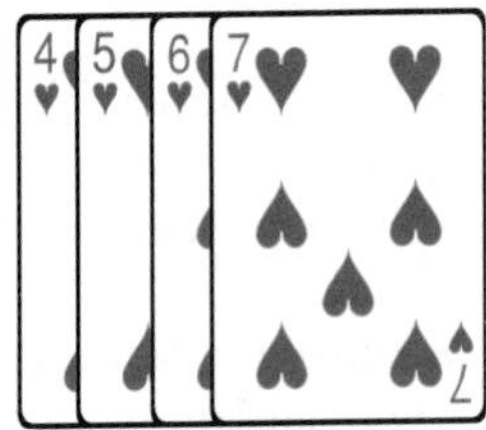

Long spreads

opponent's spread, that's considered your discard. When your spread is hit by your opponent, you must discard from your hand instead of plucking a new card!

You may shift your own melds around to create new melds as long as you leave only valid melds. For example, a ♥7 may be removed from a long spread shown in the illustration and added to two other sevens, creating a three-card set.

If you go coon can (have 11 cards in revealed spreads), the game ends and you win the agreed stake. Occasionally, if the stock is exhausted and no one goes coon can, you have a tab game, and the stake for it is added to the next game.

Coon Can's terminology:

Hit (noun): A card laid off on a meld.

Hit (verb): To lay a card off on a meld.

Hole: A hand you can't go coon can with.

Long spread: Suit sequence meld.

Pluck: To pick a card from the stock.

Short spread: Meld of the same rank.

Sleep it: To purposely overlook a play.

Switch: To move a card from one meld to another.

Tips: A good amount of skill is involved in hitting your opponent with the intent of forcing a discard from his or her hand. This discard may be a card you can use, or it may spoil your adversary's plans. Also, you may be able to force your opponent into a hole—a hand that can't go coon can. For instance, a hand that's a ten-card-long spread (a spread of an entire suit, for example) can't go coon can, since an eleventh card is required.

Sleeping it: Discarding a card that could match one's own spread may often be a good strategy, but it can be stopped. When you see your opponent sleeping it, you may force your opponent to hit with it instead, forcing a further discard.

Variations: People who are uncomfortable with placing a 7 and jack in sequence may instead use a

40-card pack, aces through 10s, removing all face cards.

Some games permit players to pluck a card just on speculation, rather than requiring it to be immediately melded or added to a spread.

♠ ♦ ♣ ♥

Crazy Eights

♠ ♦ ♣ ♥

Eights are wild and so is the action in this fast-paced game the whole family can play. An easy-to-learn game that calls for a lot of luck, Crazy Eights is an excellent game to play with kids.

Number of players: Two to six. Even more can play, but the more players, the longer each person has to wait between turns.

Object: To be the first player to go out, that is, get rid of all your cards.

The cards: A regular pack of 52 cards is used, but with four or more players you might want to use two packs.

To play: Deal seven cards to each player, turn one card up to start a discard pile, and leave the rest of the cards next to the pile as a draw stack. The player at dealer's left begins by covering the upcard with a matching card—one that's either the same suit or

To match the ♣ 6, play the ♣ 4, the ♣ 2, or the ♦ 6. Save the ♣ 8 for when you need it.

same rank. For example, if the starter is ♦ 7, any diamond or any 7 can be played. Whenever you can't match, draw cards until you find a match.

All 8s are wild and can be played at any time. Call the 8 any suit; the next player must match it. (Don't specify a rank.)

Play rotates to the left, as each player matches the top card, and continues until one player has no cards left. If you run out of draw cards along the way, simply turn over the discard pile, shuffle well, and use it for a new face-down draw pile.

Scoring: Whoever goes out scores the point total of cards left in everyone else's hands. Each 8 counts 50, face cards count 10, and all others count their face value (ace counts 1 point). The game usually ends after an agreed time limit or number of deals.

Double Crazy Eights

If your family has become crazed for Crazy Eights, you're probably ready for this new twist on an old favorite!

To play: The rules are the same as in Crazy Eights, but you turn the upcard sideways so that two piles can fit on it side by side. As play goes on, you may choose which pile to play on. You may still play an 8 anytime, but the next player must match the suit of the 8 you have played.

Tip: In Double Crazy Eights you have one more element to consider in playing. Example: You think your opponent has no diamonds and one of the piles has a diamond on top. If you can place a diamond on top of the other pile, you might force your opponent to draw cards.

Cribbage

Cribbage is thought to have been invented in the 17th century by Sir John Suckling. It was the favorite card game of Mr. and Mrs. Benjamin Franklin.

Number of players: Two

Object: To score points by forming certain card combinations and to be first to reach 121 (or 61) points.

The cards: A regular pack of 52 cards is used. Each card has a point value equal to its rank. Aces are low and count 1. Face cards count 10.

The Cribbage board: The board has 30 holes in each of four rows, marked off in groups of five. Each player gets two pegs. Begin with the four pegs at the start end of the board. The pegs move up the outside row and down the inside row back to the start, for a total of 61 points. The usual game is two trips, or 121 points. The two pegs are used alternately, the back peg leapfrogging over the front peg. If you do not have a Cribbage board, use paper and pencil to keep score.

To play: Deal six cards each, one at a time. Both players select two cards to discard together. These cards are put face down to form a four-card crib belonging to the dealer.

Next, nondealer cuts the pack and dealer turns up the top card. This is the start card. If the start card is a jack, dealer pegs 2 (scores 2 points).

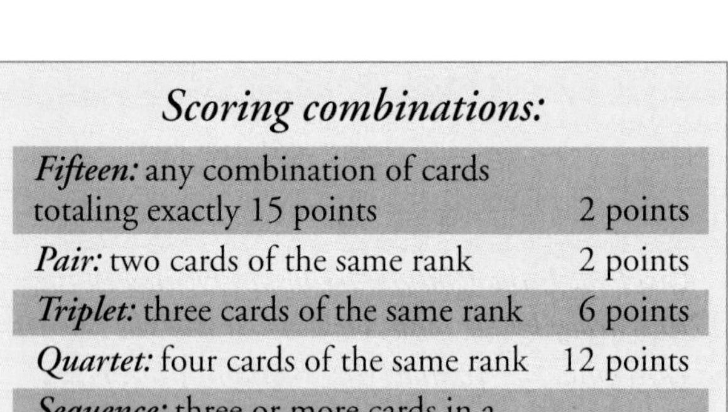

Scoring combinations:

Fifteen: any combination of cards totaling exactly 15 points	2 points
Pair: two cards of the same rank	2 points
Triplet: three cards of the same rank	6 points
Quartet: four cards of the same rank	12 points
Sequence: three or more cards in a row, any suit (aces always low)	1 point per card
Flush: four cards of the same suit	1 point per card
Jack of the start card's suit:	1 point

Nondealer now plays any one card from hand face up, calling out its value. Dealer does the same, calling out the total of the two cards played. The two players continue back and forth in this way without exceeding 31. If you cannot play without going past 31, say "Go," which instructs your opponent to continue playing as many cards as possible without going past 31. Opponent pegs 1 for your go if able to play under 31. A player who reaches 31 exactly pegs 2 points. One more point is pegged by whoever plays the last card. When both players are unable to play, a new count is started by the player who did not make the most recent play.

Pegging for melds made in play: In addition to the scoring for go, 31, and last card, combinations made during play score points. If your play makes the count

15, score 2. If you match the rank of the card played by opponent, score 2 for the pair. Three cards of the same rank are worth 6 points, and the fourth one scores 12. Sequences also count, and the cards don't have to be in exact order. For example, 3-6-4-5 scores 4 points for the last player, and if the next player follows with a deuce, that sequence is worth 5 points. A flush (series of cards of the same suit) does not score in play; it scores only when scoring the hand. Cards must be played consecutively within one 31-count to score.

Scoring the hands: After the cards have been played out, each player's hand and dealer's crib are counted

The cards you choose for the crib depend a lot on whose crib it is. If it's opponent's crib (left), keep both fives and put the 10 and 3 in the crib (or the 10 and the 8). If it's your crib, you are happy to put the 8-7 "15 combination" in the crib, keeping the 10 in your hand with both fives.

and scored. Nondealer's hand pegs first, then dealer's. The start card is scored as a fifth card in each hand.

By custom, nondealer now gathers up all the cards except the crib and the start. Dealer then turns up the crib and pegs its score. With a crib of 10-3-7-8 and a start card of 9, dealer would say, "15-2 and a four-card run makes 6."

The play of the cards can take different paths. Nondealer might start with the ♦ 2. Dealer plays ♠ 2, saying, "Four for two," and pegging two for the pair. Nondealer plays ♦ K, bringing the count to 14. Dealer can now play the ♥ A and reach 15 for 2 points, but the better play is the ♥ K, saying, "24 for two," (another pair). Nondealer plays the ♥ 4, for 28, and dealer plays ♠ 3 bringing the count to exactly 31, which scores another 2. Nondealer then starts the count again with the ♣ A, saying, "One," and dealer plays the ♥ A, saying "Two for two (another pair!), and one for last card." Dealer has pegged 9 points in play!

Pegging out: As soon as one player pegs to 121 (or 61, in a shorter game), the game ends. If you win by more than 60 points (a skunk), score for a double game.

Tips: One of the fine arts of Cribbage is choosing which cards to put into the crib and which cards to keep. If you have a high-scoring four-card group, such as 7-8-8-9, keep them and put the other two in the crib.

If it's your own crib, put scoring cards such as pairs and 15s (or at least a 5-spot) into the crib, when this also leaves you a reasonable hand. In general, put middle-range cards (4 through 8) in your own crib, and put high and low cards (2s and kings) in your opponent's. Take into account how many start cards will be good for the various choices of cards to keep. Likewise, consider how different start cards can combine with your crib discards.

In play, start with a card that counts under 5 so that opponent can't peg an immediate 15.

Near the end of the game, scoring order can greatly influence your discards and your decisions in play. For example, if you need just 3 or 4 points to win, then you don't need a high-scoring hand. Try to keep cards that will permit you to win during the play-out.

Similarly, when dealer is 5 or 10 points from winning, opponent needs to score points soon and may have to gamble on getting help from the start card for a high-scoring hand.

♠ ♦ ♣ ♥ ♠ ♦ ♣ ♥ ♠ ♦ ♣ ♥ ♠ ♦ ♣ ♥ ♠ ♦

Demon

♠ ♦ ♣ ♥

This is a solitaire game played by many people at once, with everybody building on common piles. Action and noise can reach high levels, so you may need to keep a whistle handy!

Number of players: Two to eight
Object: To play out more cards than any other player.
The cards: Each player uses a regular pack of 52 cards with a different back design.
To play: Each player deals a layout for the solitaire Klondike (see page 222). At a signal, turn over three cards from stock to start your waste heaps, and begin making plays.

There are several moves available to you. You should release your aces into the center of the table as soon as possible, where any player can build them up in sequence by suit, ending with the king. These piles are called foundation piles.

You can build downward sequences on the cards in your layout, in alternating suit color only. For example, the ♦10 can be moved upon the ♠J, but not on the ♥J. Play cards onto the center foundation piles as available. Note that everyone can play onto each foundation pile, but each player can build only onto his own layout.

When you move a card from its pile, turn up the card beneath. Occasionally a pile empties, opening up a vacancy. You can fill this only with a king or with a sequence headed by a king.

The topmost card of your waste heap is always available for play, as is any single card on a pile, and also the topmost (lowest) card of a sequence.

In the illustrated hand, move the ♥A to the center of the table to start a foundation pile. Move the ♦8 onto the ♣9 and both onto the ♦10. Now turn up the four exposed face-down cards.

When you've gone through the stock three cards at a time, turn your waste heap over to make a new stock. You can continue to do this as often as you like. At some point you may run out of plays, but as other players develop their layouts, your cards may become eligible to play in the center, and you may find several more plays.

The game ends when one player's cards have all been played into the middle foundation piles. That player shouts "Demon!" and all further play ceases. The cards on the foundation piles are then sorted out to return to each respective player. (The game is also considered complete when no player can find a play.)

Scoring: A player going out scores 52 points plus a ten-point bonus, and everyone else gets one point per card in the foundation piles. One player keeps a tally for everyone, and at the end of an agreed-upon number of deals the winner is the one with the highest total score.

Note: Not infrequently, two players will attempt to play the same card on the same foundation pile. Whoever's card is at the bottom is deemed to have arrived there first.

♠ ♦ ♣ ♥

Durock

♠ ♦ ♣ ♥

This popular Russian game of attack and defense uses trumps in a most unusual way. Durock, incidentally, means "fool!"

Number of players: Two or more, but this is an especially good game for five players.

Object: Not to be Durock, the last player left with cards.

The cards: One regular pack of 52.

To play: Deal five cards to each player. Turn up the next card, which designates the trump suit. Leave it visible but under the rest of the undealt cards, the stock (or talon). Aces are high.

Play consists of a clockwise progression of attack and defense. Attacker plays one to five cards on the table. The next player defends the attack with two options: Either pick up and keep the attacking cards, or else beat each attack card.

The attack: The attack may be any of these plays: a single card, a pair (two cards of the same rank), three of a kind (three cards of the same rank), two pairs, four of a kind (four cards of the same suit), or a full house (a pair plus 3 of a kind).

To defend, you must beat each card in the attack by a higher card in the same suit or by a trump card.

Joining the attack: Other players may add, at any time, more cards of the same rank as an attack card. At no time may the total number of attack cards be larger than 5, however. In the example hand, any other player could add to the attack with a 4 or a 9. Since the attack must stop with 5 cards, this time only one player can add to the attack. For example, if Victor adds the ♦ 9, Jill will have to top it with a higher trump, or else pick up all the cards. Note that attack cards up to a limit of five can still be thrown even as defender is picking up the earlier part of the attack.

If the defender beats every attack card, then all cards involved are retired from play.

Replenishing hands: Starting with attacker and including defender, all players with zero to four cards now draw from the talon until each has five cards again. Any player with 5 or more cards does not draw.

Ongoing play: If successful, the defender now becomes the new attacker. If the defender picked up

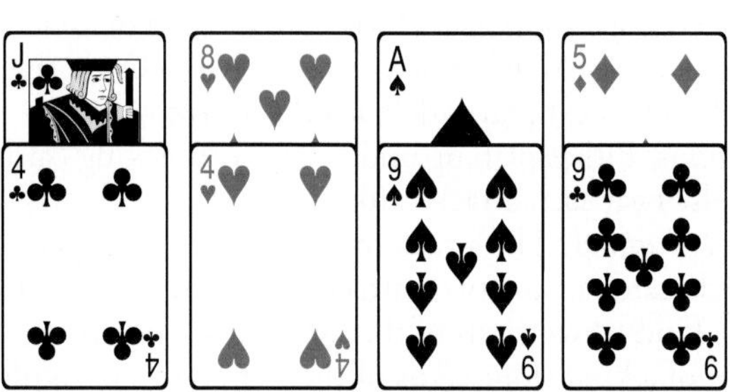

In the hand shown, ♦s are trump and Eddie has attacked Jill with ♣4 ♥4 ♠9 ♣9. Jill could have picked up these cards, but her hand happens to be good enough to beat each: She plays ♣J ♥8 ♠A ♦5, topping each attack card with a higher card in that suit or with a trump.

cards, then the following player makes the next clockwise attack.

Play continues like this until the talon is exhausted. (The trump upcard is the last card drawn.) Here's when the fun really begins! Now, as soon as you have no cards left, you're out of the hand and you can't be Durock; you can relax and watch the others play.

When only two players remain, if one attacks using all their remaining cards, the other player is Durock without getting a chance to defend.

By tradition, Durock takes on the shame of gathering, shuffling, cutting, and dealing the cards for the next hand. Also by tradition, if someone other than Durock touches the cards, that person becomes dealer!

Note: At the end of the hand, a player with fewer than five cards can be attacked only up to the number

of cards held. Example: Victor has 3 cards. Hugo attacks him with 2 cards, as Jill adds a third. Eddie cannot join the attack. Victor picks up those cards, and now that he has 6 cards, he may receive a full attack the next time.

Scoring: If you are playing for a stake, Durock pays one chip to each other player.

Tips: It does not hurt to pick up attack cards in the early stages. You'll still have chances to get rid of many of these cards before players start to drop out. In fact you can gather high cards of the same rank, such as three kings, and use them to counter an attack. If you have trumps, especially high ones, they will be most helpful in the endgame. Also, when your right-hand opponent is defender, by withholding from the attack, or by adding to it, you may influence whether he or she succeeds or fails.

Variations: In a large game, the right to join the attack may be limited to the players nearest the attacker.

Pass-the-buck: Under this rule, the defender who can match the attack card passes the attack along onto the next player, who takes over as defender. Example: Meg is attacked with ♠6. Meg plays ♣6 and passes the pair of 6s along to the next player, Stan, who becomes the defender.

A popular traditional Durock variant limits the initial attack to one rank, but any new card defender plays opens up that rank for attack too. Example: ♦s are trump. Hugo plays ♥5 at Victor. Victor plays ♥7 to beat the attack, but then Hugo extends the attack by playing the ♣7, while Eddie tosses on the ♠7!

Victor may want to pick up the pile now, before it gets any bigger!

Durock with six cards dealt is a popular form of the game. Also, some prefer to play with a 36-card pack created by removing all 2s through 5s.

♠ ♦ ♣ ♥

Eleusis

♠ ♦ ♣ ♥

Over four decades ago, Robert Abbott developed this unusual card game. Nowadays, other versions exist, but this one, close to the original, is one of the most inviting.

Number of players: At least three

Object: To get rid of as many cards as you can by discovering the rule of play governing the hand.

The cards: A regular pack of 52 cards.

To play: Dealer turns the top card up as a starter, then deals the whole pack out to the other players—dealer gets no cards. Dealer now writes down a secret rule of play, simple or complicated, guiding the cards players may legally discard from their hand onto the starter pile. Dealer puts the secret rule out of sight until the end of the hand.

At your turn, you must play at least one card on the

discard pile. Dealer says, "Right," if your play follows the rule. Then the next player goes. However, if your play is illegal, dealer says, "Wrong," and you must leave any cards played face up in front of you, where they still count as part of your hand. You may try playing these exposed cards later. If your play contains a series of cards, each one in turn must be a correct play.

In the example below, with the start card the ♦10, dealer's rule was if the card is even and red, play a heart; if the card is even and black, play a diamond; if the card is odd and red, play a spade; and if the card is odd and black, play a club (jack and king are considered odd, queen is even). All cards added on must comply with the rule, though players may still not have figured out why!

Game is over when one player has no cards, either in hand or on the table. Game also may end when dealer affirms that no player has a legal play and the game is blocked (dealer may show the written rule at this point). The winner is the first to play out all his or her cards, or, in a blocked game, the one with the fewest cards left. Deal rotates to the left for each new hand.

Scoring: Losers double the difference between the number of cards they hold and the number the winner has left (if any). Winner and dealer split

these winnings equally. Example: In a four-player game, the winner has two cards left while first loser has three and second loser has nine. First loser scores −2, second loser scores −14, and winner and dealer each score +8. In case two players tie for the fewest cards, dealer still receives half the losing sums, while the winners share what's left. Since dealer always wins, be sure everybody gets an equal number of deals.

Tips: Since as dealer you get your best score when one player figures out the rule and can get way ahead of the other players, use your judgment of the other players to design a rule one of them may figure out more quickly than the others.

Here are two examples of rules you can use: (1) If the card is a diamond, play any other suit; if the card is a club, play a red card; if the card is a spade, play a black card; if the card is a heart, play a card of the same rank. (2) If the sum of the last two cards played is 2–8, play a spade; if the sum of the cards is 9–12 play a club; if the sum is 13–16 play a diamond; if the sum is 17 or more, play a heart (picture cards count 10, Ace = 1).

Euchre

♠ ♦ ♣ ♥

Euchre is thought to have descended from a popular sixteenth-century game. A hundred years ago in America, it had plenty of devotees and was considered our national game!

Number of players: Four, with partners seated facing each other. Euchre may also be played by two or three players.

Object: To score points by winning at least three of five tricks.

The cards: A 32-card pack, 7s through aces for each suit, is used. All 2s through 6s are discarded before play. Cards rank as follows: A-K-Q-J-10-9-8-7, except in trumps, where the jack (called the right bower) is high, and the other jack of the same color (the left bower) is the second highest trump.

To play: Deal five cards to each player, in bunches of two and three, or three and two, and turn up the next card to propose a trump suit. If that suit becomes the trump suit, the upcard replaces another in dealer's hand. By custom, it stays on the table, while the card it replaces is put beneath the remaining undealt cards.

Determining the trump suit: Starting at dealer's left, each player has a chance to accept or pass the suit turned as trumps. To accept, an opponent of the dealer says "I order it up," dealer's partner says

"I assist," and dealer accepts by discarding. Any player may pass.

On balance, to accept you should judge your side at least a two-to-one favorite, since you win only one point when you succeed (unless you score a march), but lose two points when you fail (see "Scoring").

If all four players pass, dealer places the upcard under the pack of undealt cards, and another round follows to find a trump suit. Starting with the player at dealer's left, each may pass until one player names a trump suit other than the suit first turned up. If all players again pass, throw the cards in and shuffle for a new deal.

The hands shown form a Euchre challenge. Hearts are trumps—and the jack of diamonds is the left bower. Although dealer (right) has four trump cards and nondealer has only three, nondealer can still win three tricks. If nondealer leads ♠ K, dealer takes the trick with ♥ 8. Dealer then leads the left bower, ♦ J, and nondealer takes it with ♥ J. Nondealer leads ♦ 7, and dealer takes it with ♥ 9. No matter which card dealer leads now, the remaining two tricks are nondealer's.

Scoring:	
Declaring side wins three or four tricks	1 point
Declaring side wins five tricks (a march)	4 points
If lone hand wins	4 points
Declaring side euchred (wins fewer than three tricks), opponents score	2 points

Game is played to a predetermined number of points, usually 5, 7, or 10.

When accepting or naming a trump suit, you may also declare at that time to play alone. Your partner's hand is put aside, and you play against both opponents.

The player at dealer's left usually leads to the first trick, but when you play a lone hand, the defender at your right leads first.

On each trick, follow the suit of the card led if possible. Otherwise, play any card. Each trick is won by the highest card of the suit led, except a trick containing at least one trump, which is won by the highest trump played. Note that the ♥J is not considered a heart when diamonds are trumps!

Tips: The trump suit has nine cards, but there are only seven cards in the other suit of the same color. The two remaining suits have eight cards each. Since

each deal leaves out about a third of the deck, on average only five or six cards of each suit are in play. If you have three cards in the trump suit and your partner can take a trick, you are likely to win the majority of tricks.

When you have three practically certain winning cards in your hand and chances of winning the other cards, it may be wise to play alone. Your nontrump cards, even if not clear winners, may take tricks anyway: Your opponents have only ten cards between them and may fail to hold on to the right cards!

Don't forget that if the upcard is accepted as trumps, it becomes part of the dealer's hand. This may influence your decision to accept that suit as trumps for your side.

The game score may also influence your decision to pass, accept, or play alone. If you have a large lead, it may be a good risk to venture a questionable acceptance of the trump suit if you fear an opponent may score a march (4 points) in a different suit. Even if you're euchred, opponent scores only 2 points.

Variation: Two-Handed Euchre is generally played with a 24-card pack, omitting 7s and 8s as well. Score for a march is 2 points.

♠ ♦ ♣ ♥ ♠ ♦ ♣ ♥ ♠ ♦ ♣ ♥ ♠ ♦ ♣ ♥ ♠ ♦

Fan Tan

♠ ♦ ♣ ♥

Don't confuse Fan Tan—also known as Card Dominoes, Sevens, and Parliament—with Chinese Fan Tan, an unrelated gambling game.

Number of players: Three to eight, but the game is best when four play.

Object: To be the first to play off all your cards.

The cards: A regular pack of 52 cards is used. Aces are low.

To play: Give each player an equal supply of chips. Deal one card at a time to each player until the whole pack is dealt. It doesn't matter if some players have one card fewer than the others.

Beginning with the player at dealer's left, each player must play a 7, or else add on to cards in suit sequences ascending or descending from the 7s. Once the ♦7 has been played, for example, the ♦8 and ♦6 can be played. If the ♦8 is played, you can play the ♦9. Sequences ascend to the king and descend to the ace. Once an end card is reached, fold up the row of cards and turn them over.

Whenever you have no card to play, pass, and toss one chip into the kitty (the bowl). Whoever is out of cards first collects the chips in the kitty, plus one chip per card left in each player's hand.

Tips: Try to encourage play in suits where you have aces or kings. Your goal is to be able to hold back

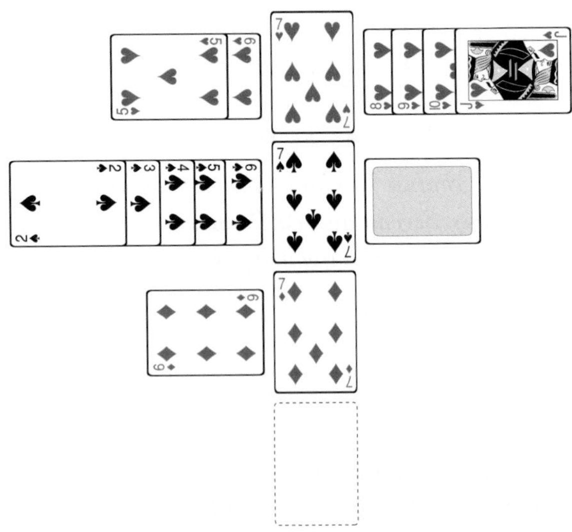

stoppers, the 5s, 6s, 8s, and 9s that block everyone else's cards but not your own. If your timing is right, the suits you need help in will open up before your stoppers are gone.

♠ ♦ ♣ ♥

Gleek

♠ ♦ ♣ ♥

Gleek used to be very popular in coffee houses—about 375 years ago! The few words written about it at the time don't give us a lot to go by, but this should give you a taste of card-playing time-travel.

Number of players: Three

Object: To make the highest scores.

The cards: A 44-card pack made by removing all 2s and 3s from a regular pack. Also, give each player an equal quantity of chips.

To play: Deal 12 cards to each player, and turn up the next card to determine the trump suit. Leave the seven remaining cards, or stock, in a face-down pile.

Each deal has four parts: (1) bidding for the stock, (2) vying for Ruff, the best suit, (3) claiming bonuses for mournivals (4 of a kind) and gleeks (3 of a kind), and (4) play of the cards.

Bidding for the stock: Player at left of dealer automatically begins the bid at 10 chips. In turn, players increase the bidding by two chips at a time, or else drop out of the bidding. The high bidder pays each opponent half the bid amount. Without revealing any cards, the high bidder then discards seven cards from his or her hand and replaces them with the stock cards.

Ruff: All players toss two chips in a pool. Starting with the high bidder, players vie for who has the best

suit (i.e., the highest total card value in a single suit): Ace counts 11, face cards 10, and all others face value. Starting with high bidder, either pass or vie for Ruff by betting two chips. Players may pass or see the vie by putting in two chips. They may also revie by adding two chips more. Once the other players have seen the vies or revies or passed, the suits are shown, and whoever has the highest count in one suit wins.

Mournival and gleek: A player with four aces receives eight chips from each other player. Four kings receive six chips, four queens receive four, and four jacks receive two. Three aces receive four chips, three kings receive three, three queens receive two, and three jacks receive one.

Trick play: The high bidder leads to the first trick. Follow suit if possible, otherwise play any card. A trick is won by the highest trump played, or else by the highest card of the suit led. Winner of each trick leads to the next.

Scoring: Score three points per trick won, plus bonuses for the following cards: ace of trumps, 15 points; jack of trumps, 9 points; king and queen of trumps, 3 points each. If the trump card turned up is one of these honors, add it to dealer's score. Now, subtract 22 points from each player's score to get the number of chips each player wins and loses!

Variations: It is common for the player having tiddie, the 4 of trumps, to claim two chips from each player. Tiddie can be claimed at any phase of the hand, and if tiddie happens to be the card turned up, dealer claims the chip reward immediately.

♠ ♦ ♣ ♥

♠ ♦ ♣ ♥ ♠ ♦ ♣ ♥ ♠ ♦ ♣ ♥ ♠ ♦ ♣ ♥ ♠ ♦

Go Fish

♠ ♦ ♣ ♥

For many of us, Go Fish was our first card game, and for some of us, it may still be the one we play best!

Number of players: Two to six

Object: To win the most sets of four cards (books) by asking other players for them.

The cards: A regular pack of 52 cards is used, but you might shorten the pack in order to have a quicker game by removing all cards of a few different ranks.

To play: When two people play, deal seven cards each; otherwise, deal five cards each. Leave the undealt cards face down as a draw pile. Starting with the player at dealer's left, each player asks another for cards of a specific rank. For example: "Kevin, do you have any 6s?" In order to ask, you must already have at least one 6. Kevin has to give you all the 6s he holds.

With this hand, you can ask for 2s, Qs, 10s, 3s, or 4s.

Whenever your request for a card is filled, it remains your turn. Continue with your turn, asking any player for cards of a specific rank. When the player you ask can't oblige, you'll be told to "Go Fish." Pick up the top card of the draw pile. If it's the rank you called for, show the card at once, and your turn goes on. Otherwise, your turn ends.

Play proceeds to the left in this fashion. Whenever you have collected all four cards of one rank (a book), show the other players, then place the book next to you in a compact pile.

Scoring: When all the cards have been drawn and all the books collected, whoever has gathered the most books wins.

Tip: Pay attention to who seeks which cards in case you draw a card someone was looking for earlier.

Variations: Call for cards from all players at once—the game moves faster when everyone must give up the wanted cards. This also makes it a better move to ask for a card when your book lacks just one, since whoever might have drawn the fourth one must give it to you. An interesting scoring variant is to assign each book a value equal to its rank. Aces would then count 11, picture cards 10, and all other cards would be worth their face value.

♠ ♦ ♣ ♥ ♠ ♦ ♣ ♥ ♠ ♦ ♣ ♥ ♠ ♦ ♣ ♥ ♠ ♦

Hearts

♠ ♦ ♣ ♥

In any of its numerous versions, Hearts is not difficult to play, but it's certainly not easy to master. An observant and calculating player will be a consistent winner.

Number of players: Two to six, but Hearts is best suited to four players.

Object: To win as few of the penalty cards (all the hearts as well as the ♠Q) as possible, or else—if the hand is strong enough—to win them all.

The cards: A regular pack of 52 cards is used. Aces are high.

To play: Deal cards one at a time until each player has 13 (if four players).

The pass: In the pass, each player sends three cards to another player. A popular method is to pass the cards to the left on the first deal, to the right on the second deal, and across on the third deal, with no pass at all on the fourth deal. The cycle then repeats. Players may not look at the cards passed to them until they have completed their own pass.

Whoever holds the ♣2 now leads it. Follow suit if possible but if you can't, play any card other than a heart or the ♠Q. Whoever plays the highest card of the suit led wins the trick and leads to the next. For example, whoever plays the highest club on the first

No matter which way the pass goes, the ♠A and ♠K are both dangerous to keep, even though you have two lower spades. Pass them both, plus the high diamond. Of course, since you'll probably take points on this hand no matter what, if you like living dangerously, pass all your diamonds and hope for the best!

trick takes the cards played to that trick and leads to the next.

Breaking hearts: You can't lead a heart until hearts have been broken—that is, until someone has discarded a heart already. However, if it's your lead and all you have are hearts, you must lead one.

Scoring: After all the tricks have been played out, count up the penalty cards you've taken. Count 1 for each heart and 13 for the ♠Q. For instance, if your tricks include the ♠Q and the ♥6, ♥7, ♥9, ♥10, and ♥K, you would receive 18 points. The other three players would somehow score the remaining 8 points. Keep a running tally. The game ends when

someone reaches 100 points or any other agreed-upon total. Whoever has the lowest score at the end is the winner.

Shooting the moon: If the tricks you win contain all the hearts and the ♠Q, this is called shooting the moon. Subtract 26 points from your score if you shoot the moon. (If you choose, instead, you may add 26 points to everyone else's score; this would end the game more quickly.)

Tips: You generally want to avoid taking tricks; however, on most hands, you'll take a few. Your main concern is always to avoid the trick that includes the ♠Q. This especially affects the pass. If you are dealt the ♠Q, you may be safer keeping it if you have at least five spades. Otherwise it may be a danger in your hand and you should pass it, for the other players will lead spades. The ♠A and ♠K are risky to keep when you are short in spades, since they may be forced to capture the dreaded ♠Q. Spades lower than the ♠Q are usually very safe to keep, since none of them can capture the ♠Q for your hand!

Sometimes it's best to pass all your cards in a short suit with no low cards, since you'd be forced to win tricks in that suit otherwise. On some hands it may be wise to pass cards in a variety of suits to increase the likelihood of everyone following suit.

If you are thinking of shooting the moon, pass away all hearts that might be losers, since suspicious players will not let you win any hearts of mid-rank if they suspect you're shooting.

Variations: There's practically an infinite number of ways that Hearts can be played, so make sure everyone

is playing by the same rules. One popular rule is that the ♠Q must be discarded at the first available opportunity. This avoids accusations of a player holding it to "dump" on a specific opponent. Another widespread rule is to count either the ♦J or ♦10 as −10 points in favor of whoever wins it.

In some games, the pass is always to the left, while some prefer no pass at all; in others, the ♣2 isn't required to be led—instead, the player at dealer's left may lead any card at all.

For three players, discard the ♦2, leaving 51 cards, and deal 17 cards to each player. Pass four cards, not three. With more or fewer than four players, you can pass left and right, but not across.

♠ ♦ ♣ ♥ ♠ ♦ ♣ ♥ ♠ ♦ ♣ ♥ ♠ ♦ ♣ ♥ ♠ ♦

Two-Handed Hearts

♠ ♦ ♣ ♥

This two player version of the four-handed game retains a lot of the sport of the original.

Number of players: Two

Object: To get the lower score. Hearts taken in tricks count 1 each, and the ♠Q taken in a trick counts 6. Or you can shoot the moon, which means you take all the hearts plus the ♠Q and score 19 for the other player.

The cards: A regular pack of 52 cards is used. Aces are high.

To play: Deal 13 cards to each player, one at a time. Put the remainder of the pack face down as the stock. Unlike the four-handed game, Two-Handed Hearts does not permit exchanging cards before play. Nondealer leads to the first trick.

You must follow suit if you are able to; otherwise, play any card. No suit is trump. The trick is taken by the higher card of the suit that is led. After each trick, both players take a new card from the stock, the winner of the trick drawing first.

Hearts may not be led until a heart has been discarded unless you have only hearts, of course.

Unlike four-handed Hearts, where the ♠Q must be discarded at the first opportunity, the two-handed version doesn't require it. The reason for the rule when more people are playing is to forestall charges of favoritism; this complaint can't arise in a two-handed game. However, if a player leads the ♠A, opponent must follow with the queen if able to. If a player leads ♠K, opponent also must follow with the queen or else win the trick with the ace if either is possible.

Play continues until all tricks have been played out, even after the stock has been exhausted.

Scoring: Players count the hearts in the tricks they have taken and score a point for each. The player who took the ♠Q in a trick scores 6 points. Low score wins after ten hands. A successful moon shot scores 19 points for the other player.

Tips: You usually want to avoid taking tricks. When you win a trick, use a high card. When you lose a trick, also use a high card—for example, play the ♣10 under the ♣J.

Deuces are especially valuable, for they let you lose the lead as long as your opponent can follow suit. Of course, once the deuce is played, the 3 becomes low in that suit.

If you void yourself in a suit, you can discard the ♠Q when that suit is led. As long as you have the queen, hold other spades as protection against your opponent's spade leads. If you do not have the ♠Q and suspect that your opponent may, lead spades lower than the queen.

To shoot the moon, a player will need enough high hearts to win every heart trick. Don't let opponent's

hearts become too strong by discarding the wrong heart. You always have to sacrifice and win at least a heart or two to stop a moon shoot.

Variations: You can incorporate a number of variants. You may count the ♦10 (some prefer the ♦J) as −5; require that clubs be led at the first trick; allow hearts to be led at any time; require the ♠Q to be played at the first opportunity; consider that playing the ♠Q does break hearts; or count the ♠Q as 13 and the ♦J or ♦10 as −10.

♠ ♦ ♣ ♥

I Doubt It

♠ ♦ ♣ ♥

I Doubt It is a hilarious game that's fun for children as well as adults. If you're the sneaky sort and have a suspicious mind, then this game is for you!

Number of players: Two or more, but it's a greater challenge with at least three players.

Object: To be the first player to get rid of all your cards.

The cards: A regular pack of 52 cards is used for two to five players. Two packs of 52 cards are used for six or more players.

To play: Deal all the cards out as evenly as possible. To save time, deal in twos or threes. In turn, players discard one or more cards, announcing them by rank. Start with aces. The player at dealer's left begins by saying, for example, "Two aces," placing two cards face down in the center of the table to begin a discard stack.

The following player announces "Deuces,"or perhaps "One deuce," and puts a single card face down on the stack. The next player announces "3s," and so on, each player stating a rank just above the previous one played. After you reach kings, start play again at aces.

At your turn you must discard, but the cards you discard don't have to be the rank called for. You might announce "Three queens" and put down two jacks and a 6 or any other three cards. Be convincing. Anyone who is skeptical can challenge you by being first to shout "I doubt it!"

Lay successive discard packets crosswise to avoid disputes. Here, a player has announced 3 kings but has been caught playing two 5s and a jack!

The challenge: If challenged, turn over your discards. If they're not what you claimed, pick up the entire discard pack. But if your cards are as announced, your challenger picks up the stack!

Note that when you use a single pack, you can discard up to four cards. With a double deck, the discard can go as high as eight cards.

Tips: Often you'll need to make a phony discard. This may be easier to do when the discard stack is low. You may get away with a one-card lie. As the pile grows, so do the risks of discarding and challenging. Also, you're sure to be challenged on your final discard. So plan ahead to have at least one card of the rank you'll need. It can be helpful to expand your hand by losing an occasional challenge.

Variation: In some games, there may be too many challenges, and you may want to bring order to them. One way to do this is to permit only the next player to say "I doubt it."

Kaluki

Spell it Kalooki, Caloochi, or Kalogghi, this double-deck Rummy game has been a longtime club favorite in America and Great Britain.

Number of players: Two to six

Object: To be the first player to go out, that is, get rid of all the cards in your hand by creating melds.

The cards: Two regular packs of 52 cards plus their four jokers are used. Jokers can be used to stand for any other card.

To play: With two to four players, deal 15 cards each. With five players, deal 13 each, and with six, deal 11 each. Then turn one card up to start the discard pile. The remaining cards form the stock. A player cannot take the upcard until he or she has made an initial meld or can use the upcard immediately in a meld. Your first meld must total at least 51 points, which can include cards you lay off on other

Value of cards in melding:

Ace	15 points
Face card	10 points
Plain card	face value
Joker	value of the card it stands for

Pick up the ♣ Q to make three queens (30 points) and use the joker for the ♥ 8 to make a sequence meld worth 21 points. The total, 51, allows you to begin melding.

players' melds, keeping in mind that you have to table at least one meld of your own.

Melds are three or more cards of the same rank (no repeated suits), or three or more cards of the same suit in sequence. Aces can be high or low, but not both. For example, ♦Q-♦K-♦A and ♦A-♦2-♦3 are valid melds, but ♦K-♦A-♦2 is not.

Before your initial meld, when it is your turn, either take the upcard if you can meld it or else take the top card from stock, meld if able, and discard. After your initial meld, you are entitled to pick the card showing and discard from your hand without melding. Whenever you meld, you may also lay off cards on your own and other players' melds.

Scoring: Each losing player pays the winner 1 point per card left in hand and 2 points per joker left in hand.

Tips: It usually doesn't take many rounds for someone to go out, so there's no real advantage to delaying your initial meld. Jokers are valuable. While they can be melded as a group for 15 points each, they are put to much better use individually.

Variations: In scoring, an alternate practice is to penalize players for the face value of the cards in their hand, with jokers counting 25 points each. One version of Kaluki counts aces as 11, not 15, so agree among the players about this beforehand. A player who goes out on a single play goes Kaluki and collects double from every player.

♠ ♦ ♣ ♥

♠ ♦ ♣ ♥ ♠ ♦ ♣ ♥ ♠ ♦ ♣ ♥ ♠ ♦ ♣ ♥ ♠ ♦

Kings in the Corner

♠ ♦ ♣ ♥

Here's a snappy game that feels like everybody's playing a single solitaire—but there's only one winner!

Number of players: Two to six

Object: To go out by playing off all your cards.

The cards: You'll need one pack of 52 cards, plus a supply of pennies or chips.

To play: Deal each player seven cards, then turn four cards face up to start layoff piles. (One king will go in each corner space shown in the diagram.) Place the remaining cards face down in the center as a draw pile.

Player at dealer's left goes first, and subsequent play moves clockwise. If you make no play, pay a chip into the pool. Otherwise, play any number of cards, as long as the plays are valid. At the end of your turn, whether you made any plays or not, draw a new card—except if you go out!

These moves are valid:

1. Playing a king in a corner.
2. Playing a card one rank lower and of opposite color on the top card of any pile. (In other

words, these piles have alternating colors.) Ace is the lowest card.

3. Moving an entire layoff pile onto another, if the bottom card of the pile moved is one lower and of the opposite color than the card you are moving it to. This may occur during your turn or as a result of the deal. For example, in the layout shown, the first player can move the ♥7 onto the ♣8. A king dealt to the layout can be moved into the corner by the first player.

4. Playing any card onto a layoff space that has become empty during play.

If you play your last card during your turn, you win.

Scoring: At the end of the game, losers pay 10 chips for each king they hold, while every other card costs one chip. Winner collects all the chips. If you prefer to score on paper, omit the penalty chips paid for passes.

Tips: Although you may have several plays to make on one turn, it may be wise to save some plays for a later round. First, if you save a play for a future round, it may spare you from paying a chip to the pool. Second, by holding back a card, you may prevent the next players from making plays they might otherwise make.

♠ ♦ ♣ ♥

♠ ♦ ♣ ♥ ♠ ♦ ♣ ♥ ♠ ♦ ♣ ♥ ♠ ♦ ♣ ♥ ♠ ♦

Klaberjass

♠ ♦ ♣ ♥

Pronounced "Klobber-yosh"—or just Klob, it is probably Hungarian in origin. It became a favorite in the United States as a one-on-one test of talent.

Number of players: Two

Object: To score points by declaring sequences and by winning high-scoring cards in tricks.

The cards: A 32-card deck, A-K-Q-J-10-9-8-7 for each suit. The rank of trump cards is different from that in the other suits. Card rank in trumps: J (high), 9, A, 10, K, Q, 8, 7. Card rank in the other suits: A, 10, K, Q, J, 9, 8, 7.

To play: Deal six cards to each player, one at a time, and turn over an upcard to propose trump.

Nondealer speaks first, saying "Pass," "Take," or "Schmeiss" (pronounced "shmice"). Take means nondealer accepts the suit turned up as trump, becoming the maker, or player responsible for making the higher score. Schmeiss is an offer to throw the hand in. If dealer accepts, the cards are thrown in for a new deal. If dealer refuses, the schmeisser must become the maker with the upcard suit as trump. If nondealer passes, dealer then must pass, accept, or schmeiss.

If you both pass on the first round, nondealer names a new trump suit or passes again. If the latter,

dealer now names a new trump suit or passes. If both pass twice, the hand is thrown in, with no redeal; the deal alternates in Klaberjass.

Once a suit has been settled on for trumps, each player is then dealt another three cards, bringing the hands to nine cards. At this time it's also customary to turn up the bottom card of the deck.

If the original upcard was accepted as trump, either player with the 7 of trump may now exchange it for the upcard.

Sequences: Before playing out the tricks, determine which player, if either, has the highest sequence. Only the player with the highest-ranking sequence may score for sequences. For sequences

Scoring:

Each player earns points by taking certain cards in tricks.

Jack of trump (Jass, pronounced "yahss")	20
9 of trump (Menel, pronounced "muh-NIL")	14
Each ace	11
Each 10	10
Each king	4
Each queen	3
Each jack (not trump)	2
Last trick	10

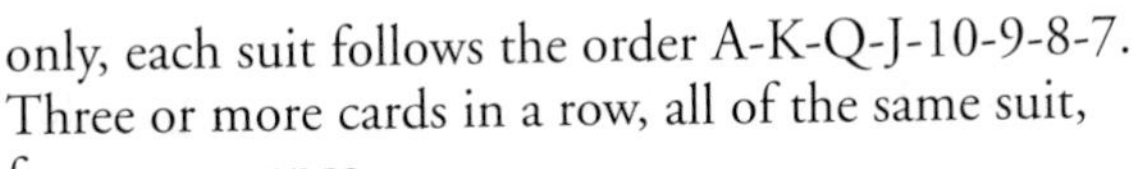

only, each suit follows the order A-K-Q-J-10-9-8-7. Three or more cards in a row, all of the same suit, form a sequence.

A three-card sequence is worth 20 points; a four-card or longer sequence is worth 50 points. A 50-point sequence is higher than a 20-point sequence. Between sequences of equal value, the one with the higher top card is higher. If the sequences tie in rank, a sequence in trump beats one not in trump. If neither sequence is trump, nondealer's sequence beats dealer's.

Nonmaker begins the dialogue, claiming "20" or "50" or "no sequence." Maker now answers, either declaring "no sequence," or agreeing that nonmaker's meld is "good," or, if the sequences have equal value, by asking, "How high?"

Your opponent (on left) passes, but you should take up, planning to exchange the ♥ 7 for the ♥ A. You'll have the three highest trumps, guaranteeing 45 points, and you are likely able to win last trick too. If the three cards you draw contain any other trumps or aces, you will do very well.

The player whose sequence is high may also declare any other sequence, regardless of its value or rank. To score your sequences, you must show them before playing to the second trick. The other player scores no sequences.

Once the sequences dialogue is over, play begins. No matter who the maker is, nondealer always makes the first lead. Thereafter, the winner of a trick leads to the next one.

A trick is won by the higher trump in it or, if it has no trump, by the higher card. You must follow suit if able. If unable to follow suit, you must trump if possible; otherwise, you may discard. If a trump is led, you must play a higher trump if able.

Bella: If you hold the K-Q of trump, declare 20 points for Bella when you play the second of them to a trick.

Players combine their trick score with any sequences or Bella. If maker's total is greater than defender's, then both record their points. If maker and defender tie, defender's score only is recorded. If defender scores more than maker, credit defender with both scores. First player to 500 points wins.

Tips: You won't always have a rock-crusher of a hand in the first six cards. The last three cards received can be high trumps and nice cards for sequences, or useless losers, or a mix of the good and the bad. If you become the maker needing to fill in an open sequence, you probably won't get it. With two sequences open, your chances improve a good deal.

J-Q-K or J-9-A of trump is an obvious take, but you may want to take with J-Q of trump plus some

high tricks. Jack alone with two outside tricks is a very reasonable take. Also, to accept with A-K-Q of trump (40 points with Bella) and an outside ace will usually win—unless opponent has very high trumps or a 50 sequence.

The schmeiss is a unique feature of Klaberjass. As nondealer, schmeiss when you have only a fair chance to win with the trump proposed and fear opponent may make a big score picking a different suit for trumps. Otherwise, pass and name a good suit later.

When nondealer passes, dealer should accept or schmeiss if possible rather than allowing opponent to name a new trump suit.

If opponent is nearing 500 and you are rather behind, don't become maker unless you have a chance to win big. Otherwise opponent will score enough points simply as defender.

Variations: Some players allow nondealer a schmeiss on the second round, after two passes. For instance, "Schmeiss clubs" leaves dealer the choice to either throw the hand in or be the defender with clubs as trump. Dealer cannot schmeiss on the second round.

♠ ♦ ♣ ♥ ♠ ♦ ♣ ♥ ♠ ♦ ♣ ♥ ♠ ♦ ♣ ♥ ♠ ♦

Knaves

♠ ♦ ♣ ♥

Looking for an entertaining game to play when you don't have a foursome? Here's an easy trick-taking game for three.

Number of players: Three

Object: To win as many tricks as possible, but to avoid winning jacks (knaves).

The cards: One 52-card pack.

To play: Deal 17 cards to each player and turn the last card up as trump. Player at dealer's left leads to the first trick. Follow suit whenever possible; otherwise trump or play any other card; you are not required to trump if you don't have the suit led. The winner of a trick leads to the next trick.

Scoring: After all 17 tricks have been played, score one point for each trick taken. For each jack taken, you subtract points. The first to reach a score of 21 wins.

Avoid these cards, which score -4, -3, -2, and -1 points, respectively.

Tip: When you play second to a trick in a suit where the jack is still out, playing the Q, K, or A is taking a big chance. But as third and last to play, you may want to win a trick with the Q, K, or A—even when you could do so with a much lower card. This saves you the risk of taking the jack on a later play.

Variation: Some use a rule that when the turned-up trump card is a jack, it goes to the winner of the last trick.

Leopard

This is an unusual and challenging game of changing spots.

Number of players: Two

Object: To score cards in lines of three of the same color.

The cards: Use two decks of 52, 104 in all.

To play: Deal eight cards to each player. Place the rest of the cards in a draw pile, with room for a discard pile next to it.

Each player lays out a three-by-three grid like the one in the diagram on the next page. Note: there will be one open space at the start.

The grid in the diagram is worth 8 points before bonus: It has two single-suit lines, worth 4, plus four lines of mixed suits of the same color, worth 4 more points. With bonus, the score for the hand is 11.

Starting with nondealer, take one card from the draw pile, and then play one card onto either your grid, your opponent's grid, or the discard pile.

Legal moves: Playing an A through 9 in appropriate spot on either player's grid only if that spot is empty.

Playing a 10 on any empty space in your own grid.

Playing a jack face down on any card in either your grid or opponent's. (Note: A face-down card on a spot makes it empty again.)

Playing a queen face down on any card in your grid only.

Playing a king face up on any card or in any empty space, only in your own grid.

Discarding onto the discard pile. Discards may not be picked up by either player. If discarding a queen or jack, you must place it in the discard pile face up.

Going out: You may go out or you may stop play when your square has a value of 5 or more. You may go out only when it is your turn to play or discard a card. You may not go out after you play or discard, but you must wait until it is your turn to play again.

If no one goes out and you exhaust the stock, play on with the cards you have left. If all cards are played and still no one has gone out, players score whatever value their squares have.

Scoring: A grid line with three cards of all the same suit scores 2 points. A line with cards of all the same color, but mixed suits, scores 1 point. Verticals, horizontals, and diagonals all count, so there are eight lines in all. Your grid can score both red-suited lines and black-suited lines, but the more cards of one color you have in your grid, the higher your score is likely to be. If no one goes out, for every point over 5 that your square is worth, score one additional point. The penalty for going out is 1 point; subtract it from the value of the grid.

Record each player's score. Players alternate deal, and a game consists of four deals.

♠ ♦ ♣ ♥ ♠ ♦ ♣ ♥ ♠ ♦ ♣ ♥ ♠ ♦ ♣ ♥ ♠ ♦

Tips: Because you can play jacks anywhere to interfere with your opponent's plans, they are very valuable cards. If possible, save them for important occasions. For example, they are the only cards you can play on an opponent's king. When playing a jack onto opponent's grid, pick a spot where there may be a weakness.

Variation: Running Leopard is played by drawing two cards at a time instead of one. You must still at least discard one card, but if you play on the grids, you may play as many cards as you like as long as each is legal. Score as in regular Leopard.

♠ ♦ ♣ ♥

Michigan

♠ ♦ ♣ ♥

The many names of this game—Chicago, Saratoga, Newmarket, Stops, Boodle, and others—show its far-reaching appeal. Though played with cards and chips, it doesn't involve betting.

Number of players: Three to eight

Object: To win chips by being the first player out of cards and by playing money or boodle cards.

The cards: A regular pack of 52 cards is used, plus an extra ♥A, ♣K, ♠Q, and ♦J (the boodle cards). Aces are high.

To play: Distribute an equal number of chips to each player. (Number agreed upon by players). Place the four boodle cards face up in the center of the table, where they remain throughout play. Each player puts one chip on each boodle card except the dealer, who places two chips on each.

Deal all the cards out, one at a time, dealing one hand more than there are players. The extra hand, called the widow, is dealt to dealer's left. It's all right if some players have one more card than others.

As dealer, look at your cards and decide if you wish to exchange them for the widow (without seeing it first). If you prefer, keep your original hand and auction the widow, still unseen, to the other players. The auction begins at one chip. The high bidder wins the widow hand and must play it and pay the dealer.

The player at dealer's left leads the lowest card held of any suit. Whoever has the next card in sequence in

This hand lacks boodle cards, high cards, and aces. Consider swapping it for the widow.

that suit plays it, and so on, until no one can play. For example, the ♥4 is led, the same player also plays the ♥5, and then other players follow with the ♥6, ♥7, and ♥8. No one has the ♥9, a stopper, so whoever played the ♥8 now continues play, leading the lowest card of a different suit.

When an ace is played, the sequence ends. Begin a new sequence with your lowest card in another suit. Whenever you play a boodle card, collect the chips on it. If you play your last card, the deal ends and you win; collect one chip from each player for every card remaining in their hand. The deal also ends when no one can continue the sequence and the last player lacks another suit to lead.

Leave all uncollected chips on the boodle cards. The deal passes to the left, and all players put another chip on each boodle card. Since the dealer has an advantage, the game ends after an agreed number of complete dealing rounds. Whoever has the most chips is the winner.

Tip: If you take the widow, remember the cards you threw away. This can help a lot in the play.

Variations: One version of Michigan requires that players pay an extra penalty if they are caught at the end holding a boodle card. Another variant adds a fifth boodle, usually the sequence ♥9-♥10-♥J. Anyone playing two of these cards in a row collects their boodle chips. You can always use an A-K-Q-J of different suits for boodle cards, but if you use the 9-10-J sequence boodle, it should be the same suit as the ace.

♠ ♦ ♣ ♥

♠ ♦ ♣ ♥ ♠ ♦ ♣ ♥ ♠ ♦ ♣ ♥ ♠ ♦ ♣ ♥ ♠ ♦

Molimba

♠ ♦ ♣ ♥

This is a quick game of taking and losing tricks that may feel at times like a tug-of-war.

Number of players: Two

Object: To reach molimba—a hand with cards of two suits only.

The cards: A regular pack of 52 cards is used.

To play: Deal nine cards to each player and two cards, called the shed, face down on the table. Put the rest of the cards aside.

Nondealer leads the first trick. You must follow suit if possible, otherwise play any card (there's no trump suit). Ace is the highest card in each suit. If you win the trick, then pick up both cards and add them to your hand. If you lose the trick, discard two cards, and then pick up the shed. The discards are the new shed.

After picking up the shed, if you have only two suits left, you have molimba, and the hand ends. But if you have cards of three or more suits, play continues, with the winner of the last trick leading to the next. As before, the winner takes the cards, and the loser gets to exchange with the cards in the shed.

Scoring: Basic molimba scores 10. Multiply the basic score times 2 for black molimba (suits are ♣ and ♠), times 3 for red molimba (suits are ♦ and ♥), times 3 for pat molimba (being dealt molimba), and times 4 if you have solid molimba (just one suit).

Play to 200 points.

The highest scoring hand possible is nine cards dealt in a red suit—solid pat red molimba—360 points (10 x 4 x 3 x 3). It is very rare.

Tips: Occasionally someone gets molimba after the first or second play, but usually it requires strategy in using the shed. Often, you can plan a play ahead. For instance, if you expect to lose two tricks in a row, you can use the first trick lost to put cards in the shed that you'll be getting back right away, since you plan to lose the next trick too. That may help you get molimba: Remember, your hand has become smaller since you also lost two cards on those losing tricks.

In contrast, when you lose one trick but think

First play: Ned leads.

Second play: Mary leads.

you'll be winning the next one, then put cards in the shed your opponent won't like.

Variation: For an even quicker game, deal eight cards each, but if you want to slow it down, deal ten.

♠ ♦ ♣ ♥

Nap or Napoleon

♠ ♦ ♣ ♥

The emperor Napoleon Bonaparte was neither the inventor nor the popularizer of this game, but his name is used for one of the bids. Two of his enemies, Wellington and Blucher, are also bids.

Number of players: Two to five

Object: To outbid the other player and then to win the number of tricks you've bid for.

The cards: A regular pack of 52 cards is used. Aces are high.

To play: Dealer deals five cards each in groups of three and then two. Starting at dealer's left, each player must make one bid, naming a number of tricks to be won. The bid does not name desired trump suit, only the number of tricks.

A Misère bid outranks a bid of 3. Napoleon, Wellington, and Blucher are all bids to take all five tricks, but each scores differently. This means that a player who bids Napoleon for five tricks can be outbid by another player bidding Wellington, which can be outbid by a Blucher.

First player must bid 2 or pass. If all pass, throw the hand in. High bidder becomes the maker. Maker's opponents work together to try to make the bid fail.

Maker begins by leading a card to the first trick. This card's suit becomes trump, except, of course, if the bid is Misère, which is no trump. You must follow suit when you are able to; otherwise you may trump or discard. A trick is won by the highest trump in it or, if it contains no trump, by the highest card in the suit led. The winner of each trick leads to the next.

Scoring: Maker wins or loses points to each opponent. Enter the plus or minus scores after every deal.

Bids in Nap:

1	1 trick
2	2 tricks
3	3 tricks
Misère (mee-ZAIR)	3 tricks, no trump suit
4	4 tricks
Napoleon	5 tricks
Wellington	5 tricks
Blucher	5 tricks

Be sure the scores always add up to zero.

If as maker you win the number of tricks you bid, score the number of points you bid. Nothing extra is scored for overtricks. If you bid and make Napoleon, Wellington, or Blucher, score 10 points.

The opponents score for defeating maker's bid. If maker doesn't take the number of tricks bid, opponent scores that number. Opponents score 5 for defeating Napoleon, 10 for defeating Wellington, and 20 for defeating Blucher. It's the risk of greater loss that separates the three different bids for all five tricks.

Nap is a fast game to play. The first to reach 30 points is the winner.

♠ ♦ ♣ ♥

Oh Hell!

♠ ♦ ♣ ♥

In Oh Hell! it's not how good your cards are, but how good your luck and judgment are. The game does have its momentary upsets, so if you need a name that's a bit more tame, just call it "Oh Well!".

Number of players: Three to seven; however, the game is best with four or five players. One player should be scorekeeper.

Object: To make precisely the number of tricks you bid—no more, no less.

The cards: A regular pack of 52 cards is used. Aces are high.

To play: A game of Oh Hell! consists of a series of rounds. On the first, deal each player one card; on the second, deal two cards; and on the third, deal three, increasing the deal by one card each hand until the top limit. For example, when four people play, deal 13 cards on the last round. With five players, deal ten cards on the last round. The deal goes to the left for each new round.

After dealing, turn up one card to designate trumps. If you turn over an ace or a deuce, however, play at no-trump, with no suit as trumps. Also, whenever you deal all 52 cards, play at no-trump.

The bidding: Starting at dealer's left, players state in turn the number of tricks they hope to win. The scorekeeper records each bid. The total number of tricks bid for on each deal must differ from the number of tricks available. Therefore, the scorer must require the last bidder—the dealer—to register a legal bid.

Once all the bids are recorded, the player at dealer's left leads any card desired. Always follow suit if possible, but play any card otherwise. Each trick is taken by the highest card in the suit led or by the highest trump. The winner of each trick leads to the following trick.

Scoring: After all the tricks have been taken, the scorekeeper tallies how everyone fared. If you made your bid exactly, score 1 point per trick plus a

10-point bonus. If you failed, however, subtract 10 points for each trick you're off, whether it's more or less than your bid. The player with the most points after the last deal wins.

Tips: Bidding in the first few rounds can be tricky, since so few cards from the pack are in play, and some bids are forced. In the early deals, you'll be surprised to see your low cards win tricks, while your aces get trumped. In most deals, you can count on low cards to be losers more reliably than counting on high cards to be winners.

When the bid total is above the number of tricks in the deal, other players will be quite willing to capture your questionable middle-range cards or trump a trick in which you played a high card. When the bid total is under the trick total, players will let you win an extra trick or two.

Variations: Some players prefer to write down bids secretly. In this case, it's okay for the bid total and the trick total to turn out equal. Those bids can be revealed either before the first lead or after the last trick.

In many games, once the highest possible number of cards have been dealt, the game continues with the number of cards per hand decreasing by one each hand, until you work your way back down to a final one-card deal.

♠ ♦ ♣ ♥ ♠ ♦ ♣ ♥ ♠ ♦ ♣ ♥ ♠ ♦ ♣ ♥ ♠ ♦

Old Maid

♠ ♦ ♣ ♥

Some 150 years ago, the ancestral form of Old Maid most likely used a regular pack minus one card.

Number of players: Three or more is best, though two can play.

Object: Not to be left holding the Old Maid.

The cards: A pack of 51 cards is used, made by removing one queen from a regular pack.

To play: Deal all the cards out one at a time. Before play starts, each player shows and retires any pairs of like rank. After that, the player at dealer's left takes one card, unseen, from the player at his or her left. If this makes a pair, it is also tabled, and the player continues, taking a card from the next player to the left. When the card taken does not make a pair, play passes on to the next player, who in turn takes a card from the next player. In this way all cards eventually pair up except one queen, and the player holding it is declared Old Maid.

Tip: After one pair of queens has been tabled, only body language can tell you who might have the remaining lone queen.

Variations: Instead of removing a queen, randomly remove one card that no one sees from the pack. In this way, only at the very end will all the players discover which card in actuality was the Old Maid.

♠ ♦ ♣ ♥

♠ ♦ ♣ ♥ ♠ ♦ ♣ ♥ ♠ ♦ ♣ ♥ ♠ ♦ ♣ ♥ ♠ ♦

Panguingue

♠ ♦ ♣ ♥

Panguingue, or Pan, a gambling game especially popular out West, can also be enjoyed as a party game. It grew out of Coon Can and uses the same cards, only it uses more of them!

Number of players: Up to 15, though best when limited to eight.

Objects: To meld certain groups of cards (conditions) and be the first to go out (meld all your cards).

The cards: Five or more Coon Can packs (regular packs of 52 cards with all 8s, 9s, and 10s omitted) are shuffled together. Aces are low.

To play: Unlike in other games, in Pan the deal and play rotate counterclockwise (to the right). Deal ten cards to each player in batches of five. Leave the remaining stock in the center of the table, turning its top card over to begin a discard pile.

Dropping: Each player decides whether to drop or play after looking at his or her hand. If you drop, throw in two chips. These chips will go to the winner of the hand. Dropping is also known as going on top, because the forfeited cards are stacked at the foot of the stock. The discards don't belong to the stock and cannot be played.

If you decide to play, you must stay in until the end. The closest remaining player to dealer's right

♠ ♦ ♣ ♥ ♠ ♦ ♣ ♥ ♠ ♦ ♣ ♥ ♠ ♦ ♣ ♥ ♠ ♦

goes first. The object of play is to meld 11 cards. A meld must consist of at least three cards in a group or sequence. A sequence is any three cards of the same suit in sequence; a group is three or more cards of the same rank.

At each turn, you may take the upcard if you can meld it or add it on to a meld you already have. Otherwise, draw the top card of the stock. After drawing, table any melds you may have and discard one card.

There are two types of melds: payoff melds (conditions) and nonpayoff melds. When you lay down a condition, each active player immediately pays you according to the chart. Note that spades score double in all conditions. All 3s, 5s, and 7s are valle cards, meaning they have value. Cards of any other rank (square cards) do not have value.

Meld values:

Meld	Value
Any group of valle cards, different suits	1 chip
Any group of valle cards, same suit	2 chips (4 chips in spades)
Any group of nonvalle cards, same suit	1 chip (2 chips in spades)
Any sequence of A-2-3	1 chip (2 chips in spades)
Any sequence of J-Q-K	1 chip (2 chips in spades)

Sequences must be either low or high; for example, ♥K-♥A-♥2 is not a valid meld. ♣5-♦6-♠7 is not a valid meld either, because a sequence must be all of the same suit.

Laying off cards: You may lay off cards onto your own melds, but not onto other players' melds. Whenever you lay off an additional card on a pay spread, you are paid again by each player. Exception: Payment for extending a same-suit valle card spread is half—just 1 chip, and 2 in spades.

Switching: You can rearrange or switch your own melds in two ways: You can take the fourth of a group and use it in another meld, and you can reshape sequence melds.

Forcing: If at your turn the top discard can be laid off onto your melds, you are not obliged to take it unless another player demands that you do. This is called forcing. You must then discard.

Top: By taking one ♦J and adding the ♦7-♦Q to it, you form a rope and still have a meld of three different jacks. Bottom: Here, the cards have been rearranged to form a condition in spades! Collect two chips from every player.

Special terms in Pan:

Condition: A spread that pays to its owner.

Going on top: Dropping out before play starts.

Noncomoquers: All kings and aces.

Rope: A sequential meld.

Spread: Any meld.

Square cards: As, 2s, 4s, 6s, Js, Qs, Ks.

Valle cards: 3s, 5s, 7s.

Scoring: Whoever goes out first is the winner. Winner receives 1 chip from every player who did not drop, plus additional payment for all his conditions. In effect, then, the winner is paid twice for his or her payoff melds.

Tips: The most important decision is whether to play a hand or pay the penalty and go on top. Usually you should stay in a hand if it contains valle cards and others that may give you pay spreads. You should also stay in the game if your cards work together and your hand offers good possibilities of melding.

Variations: Panguingue houses often use a special pack: from eight Coon Can packs, one suit of spades is omitted. Sometimes an extra ♠3, ♠5, ♠7, ♠2, and ♠Q are also removed. The player with the lowest card receives the first deal, and thereafter the winner of each deal receives cards first.

♠ ♦ ♣ ♥

♠ ♦ ♣ ♥ ♠ ♦ ♣ ♥ ♠ ♦ ♣ ♥ ♠ ♦ ♣ ♥ ♠ ♦

Pinochle

♠ ♦ ♣ ♥

Pinochle developed in Europe out of the popular game Bezique. This version, commonly called Auction Pinochle, probably was invented by immigrants to America.

Number of players: Three (or four, with the dealer sitting out each deal).

Object: To score points in melds and in play.

The cards: A 48-card Pinochle pack is used. You can put one together from two standard packs by dropping all deuces through 8s. Cards rank—from high to low—A-10-K-Q-J-9.

To play: Deal 15 cards to each player. By tradition, deal in bunches of three, or one bunch of three followed by bunches of four. Deal three cards (not the last three) to a face-down widow, or kitty.

The bidding: Starting with the player at dealer's left, each player bids or passes. The lowest bid is 250 points, and bids increase by ten points thereafter. Once you pass you can't reenter the bidding, but bidders can continue raising the auction. The auction is closed once two players have passed. The aim is to score at least as many points as you bid.

The player who wins the bid becomes the bidder. If you are the bidder, turn the three widow cards face up and add them to your hand. It may be clear at this

point that your total of melds and cards taken in play won't reach your bid. You may concede at this point, losing the amount you bid.

Otherwise, table your melds, including cards from the widow, and announce a suit as trumps. If the bidder has already reached or exceeded the value of his or her bid, play ceases immediately, and he or she scores the value of the game (see "Scoring").

Your two opponents will temporarily unite in their play against you. In order to reduce your hand back down to 15 cards, choose three unmelded cards to set aside, face down, to add later to the tricks you win. Pick up your melds and lead any card to the first trick.

Melds in Pinochle:

Flush (A-10-K-Q-J of trumps)	150 points
Royal marriage (K-Q of trumps)	40 points
Plain marriage (K-Q of other suit)	20 points
Pinochle (♠Q-♦J)	40 points
100 Aces (♠A-♥A-♣A-♦A)	100 points
80 Kings (♠K-♥K-♣K-♦K)	80 points
60 Queens (♠Q-♥Q-♣Q-♦Q)	60 points
40 Jacks (♠J-♥J-♣J-♦J)	40 points
Dix (pronounced "deece") (9 of trumps)	10 points

(If you declare a flush, you may not also declare the royal marriage it contains.)

Scoring Points:

When play is over, points are counted in tricks as follows:

Ace	11
10	10
King	4
Queen	3
Jack	2
9	0
Last trick	10

Scoring Bids:

Bid	*Points*
250–290	5
300–340	10
350–390	15
400–440	25
450–490	50
500+	100
For bids over 300, spades score double.	

The winner of each trick leads to the next. You must always follow suit, and if you cannot follow to a plain suit, you must play a trump if possible. When a trump is led, play a higher trump than the previous

player if possible. Tricks are taken by the highest card of the suit led or by the highest trump if they are played. When two of the same card, say two ♣As, are played to a trick, the one played first is considered the higher of the two.

Scoring: If you make your bid, collect points from each opponent according to the scoring table opposite. If you concede, you lose points to each opponent according to the scoring table. If you play the hand and miss your bid, lose double to each opponent for going bête (pronounced bait).

Example: You bid 370 and make 405 in spades. You receive 30 points from each opponent. If you had bid 400 and made 405 in spades, you'd win 50 from each. But, if you'd bid 410 and made only 405, you'd go bête in spades and lose 100 points to each opponent.

You have 80 kings, a pinochle, and a marriage in ♠s. With ♦s as trumps, you have 160 in melds (remember, the two ♦ 9s count 10 each). You are likely to make at least 140 in cards, since you can certainly put at least two 10s away after you pick up the widow. Bid 300, willing to be pushed a bit higher. By the way, if you get playing or melding help in the widow, you might well be able to make 300 in ♠s, which scores double! (Remember, the marriage increases to 40 points.)

Tips: Don't count on the face-down widow, or kitty, to provide you with the melding help you need. There's just better than a one in six chance that one particular card will be in the widow to give you the points you may be considering. In calculating the points you'll lose in play, figure that each opponent may put a high card on your losing tricks.

As defenders, remember the cards you've seen the bidder meld that you can beat. These are cards you should be sure to win. Occasionally the bidder will have even more cards of that suit in his hand, as a side suit in addition to trumps.

Variations: Bidding practices have their own traditions. In one, after two passes the dealer must take with a bid of at least 250. In another, the dealer passes out the hand, or opens it at 290 (but not at 250) or at 320 or higher. A third treatment requires the first hand to start at 300, and it is allowed to throw the hand in for the minimum-stake loss.

♠ ♦ ♣ ♥ ♠ ♦ ♣ ♥ ♠ ♦ ♣ ♥ ♠ ♦ ♣ ♥ ♠ ♦

Partnership Pinochle

♠ ♦ ♣ ♥

This four-player version of Pinochle, sometimes called Racehorse Pinochle, includes an auction.

Number of players: Four, playing as two pairs, with partners sitting opposite each other.

Object: To be the first team to score 1,500 points.

The cards: A 48-card Pinochle deck

To play: Deal 12 cards to each player. Bidding starts at dealer's left. Bid or pass at your turn. The first bid must be at least 250, and any following bids must be a higher multiple of 10. If you pass, you may bid at a later time, but three consecutive passes end the auction. Whoever made the highest bid becomes the declarer. If all players pass, throw the hand in, unless you've decided in advance that the dealer takes it for 250 whenever the first three players pass.

Declarer names the trump suit and then receives four cards from partner. Declarer looks them over and returns four cards—which could include some of those received. Finally, all players table any melds they hold, which are then tallied for each side.

For example, you have won the bid at 350 with ♥A-10-9, ♠A-K-Q, ♦A-J, ♣A-A-Q-J, and named clubs trump. Partner passes you the ♦J, ♥A, ♣10-J. Return to partner ♦J, ♠K-Q, ♥9, worth 60 in meld, leaving you with a powerful playing hand: ♥A-A-10, ♦A-J, ♠A, ♣A-A-10-Q-J-J. Even if your melds total only 160, you should have no problem taking 190 in play. Since Pinochle has 250 points available in play, if the declaring side is more than 250 points away from its bid, it cannot possibly fulfill it. The bid is automatically set—the declaring side's melds are erased, and opponents score the value of their melds plus a 250-point bonus. Even when the bid may be within reach, declarer (without consulting partner) may decide not to play on and take an automatic set instead.

If the hand is played but the declaring side's combined total of points in melds and play falls short of the bid, then the contract is also set. In this case the declaring side's melds and trick points are erased, while opponents score their melds and the 250-point set bonus, plus whatever points they took in tricks. If the contract is fulfilled, then both sides score all their points.

Tips: You'll probably need to achieve 80 or more melding points to make any bid, and much of this depends upon how the hands wind up after the card exchange. Before sitting down, players can discuss their exchange strategies and decide what type of cards high bidder's partner should send.

Variation: Partnership Pinochle without an auction is also quite popular. Trump is determined by turning the last card up as trumps, which becomes part of dealer's hand. Players table their melds, and then

player to dealer's left makes the first play. Each side scores the points it makes in tricks and melds. First side to 1,500 wins.

An old tradition in Partnership Pinochle is that your side must take at least one trick to score its melds.

♠ ♦ ♣ ♥

Two-Handed Pinochle

♠ ♦ ♣ ♥

Two-Handed Pinochle was probably the most popular card game for two in the United States before Gin Rummy.

Number of players: Two

Object: To score the most points by melding and by taking tricks.

The cards: A 48-card Pinochle deck

To play: Deal 12 cards to each player; turn the next card up to designate the trump suit. If it's a 9, dealer scores an immediate 10 points. The remaining cards form a stock pile.

Every deal has two phases: trick-taking with melding and the endgame. To begin the first phase, nondealer leads any card; dealer may follow by playing any card—you don't have to follow suit. Each trick is won by the higher trump, or if it contains no trump, by the higher card of the suit led. If the two cards are identical, the first one played wins.

Winner of the trick tables any one of the Pinochle melds. Though a player may hold more than one meld in hand, only one melding combination may be tabled after winning a trick. Another trick must be won to make the second meld. This does not apply to the 9s of trump. The first dix can be exchanged for the upcard to get a higher trump. The second is simply shown to opponent and the 10 points scored.

A melded card may be used again in a different meld. For example, the ♠Q may be melded with the ♠K in a marriage; when a later trick is won, the same ♠Q may be melded with a ♦J in a pinochle or with ♣Q-♥Q-♦Q for 60 queens. A second marriage in spades would require a new ♠Q and ♠K. Cards melded on the table still belong to the hand of their owner and may be played to any trick. However, cards taken in tricks are out of play for the rest of the hand.

After a trick is won and any meld tabled, both players take a new card from the stock. Winner of the trick draws first and leads to the next trick.

Endgame play: When only the upcard and a single stock card are left, the winner of the trick takes the stock card, and the loser takes the upcard (which at this point will be the 9 of trump). No further melds may be made. Players return to their hands any cards melded on the table, and the winner of the last trick starts the endgame by leading any card.

In playing the tricks during the endgame, a player must follow suit if able; otherwise, the player must trump if able. When a trump is led, opponent must play a higher trump if able. The object is to take tricks with high-scoring cards.

Game is usually played to 1,000 points. If both players reach over 1,000 points on the same deal, the higher total wins.

Tips: Cards played to tricks in the first phase of the game are no longer available for melding. Play a possible melding card only if you're sure you can spare it.

Kings and queens (especially the ♠Q) are good melding cards. Retain these cards while the possibility of melding with them is still alive. Jacks are not valuable cards to keep for melding (except the ♦J). Four different jacks score only 40 points, so unless you have this meld, don't keep jacks.

If you've seen both ♦Ks, then all other kings become less valuable, since 80 kings is no longer a possible meld.

If your opponent plays a good melding card early, it's likely to be a duplicate. However, they may be missing the rest of the meld and be strapped for a play.

Use a trump in beginning play to meld some cards and free them for play, or to prevent opponent from melding. In the endgame a long trump suit will bring in several extra tricks, as well as the last trick.

In the endgame, beware the singleton ace. If opponent plays the other ace, you follow suit and lose. Play yours first.

Piquet

Piquet is over 550 years old! Legend says it was invented by a knight who fought with Joan of Arc. In 1743, Piquet was one of five games covered in a treatise on games.

Number of players: Two

Object: To outscore your opponent over six deals (a partie).

The cards: A pack of 32 cards is used. (Remove all 2s through 6s from a standard pack.) Aces are high.

To play: Deal 12 cards to each player and place the remaining eight cards in a face-down talon. Nondealer may then choose to discard from one to five cards in exchange for an equal number of cards from the top of the talon. If nondealer exchanges fewer than five cards, he may peek at those he did not take from the top five cards. Dealer may then exchange for as many cards as nondealer has left behind. The goal of both players in this exchange is to form scoring combinations (see "Declaring").

Carte blanche: When you're dealt no picture cards, you have carte blanche. Before the exchange, show your hand and score 10 points.

Declaring: After the card exchanges, the players determine who has the better scoring combinations in three categories: point, sequence, and sets, in that order.

Point: Each player finds the suit in their hand with the highest point count. The player with the higher-point suit wins one point per card in that suit. Aces count 11, face cards 10, and other cards their face value. If dealer has ♠A-♠Q-♠J-♠10-♠8 (49) , it would beat nondealer's ♦A-♦K-♦Q-♦9-♦8 (48), for a score of 5 (1 per card).

Sequence: The longest sequence in a single suit (minimum three cards) wins. If sequences are of the same length, the one headed by the higher card wins. A sequence of three cards (a tierce) scores 3. A sequence of four (a quart) scores 4. A sequence of five or more scores the number of cards plus 10.

Sets: Players count sets of three or four cards of the same rank. A player with a foursome (a quatorze)—for instance, ♦Q-♥Q-♣Q-♠Q—beats a threesome (a trio)—♥A-♣A-♠A—regardless of rank; but in sets the same size, the higher rank scores. Trios score 3 and quatorzes 14.

Nondealer begins the dialogue, starting with point. In the example given, nondealer would say "48" to which dealer would say, "Not good, 49." In each group, only the player with the winning meld scores. That player may also score for all other qualifying melds in that category. If players tie for best in a category, neither scores. For strategic reasons, you may choose not to declare a meld. This is called sinking the meld.

The play: Play to 12 tricks with no trump. Nondealer leads any card to the first trick. The highest card of the suit led wins the trick, and the winner of a trick plays to the next. In the play, score 1 point for every trick you lead to, and 1 for every trick opponent

As nondealer, throw ♠ 10-9-8 and ♥ 7, taking four talon cards and allowing you to peek at the fifth! You hope the new cards will have the missing A or K, giving you a quatorze, or else be ♣ s, to increase your chance of winning points.

leads that you win. For example, if nondealer wins the first two tricks but loses the third, nondealer has still scored the first 3 points of play. The winner of the last trick scores 1 bonus point. Whoever wins more tricks scores a 10-point bonus, but if one player wins all 12 tricks, called a capot, the bonus is 40 points. Thus, if you lead and win all 12 tricks, you score 53 (12 for the leads, 1 for last trick, and 40 for capot).

Scoring: If you score the first 30 points of a hand, you will score either the pique or repique bonus.

Repique bonus (60 points): If either player scores 30 or more points just in card combinations before opponent scores, he or she wins the 60-point repique bonus.

Pique bonus (30 points): If nondealer scores the first 30 points in card combinations and trick-taking, he or she earns a 30-point bonus for pique. Dealer cannot win pique, because nondealer automatically scores 1 for leading.

By custom, players announce their running totals throughout the hand, writing scores down at the end.

Deal alternates, with six deals constituting a Piquet partie, or game. At the end of the partie, if both players have more than 100 points, the winner gets the difference in scores, plus a 100-point game bonus. However, if the loser has under 100 points, the winner, regardless of score, gets both scores combined, as well as the 100-point game bonus. The loser is said to be rubiconed, having not crossed the "rubicon" of 100 points.

Tip: In play, much depends on who leads first. This rule affects your card-exchanging strategy. Dealer may need to keep strength in each suit to avoid giving up a capot. On the other hand, nondealer can discard all cards of a suit to increase the chance of a capot.

Variation: Instead of playing a Piquet partie, play Piquet au Cent, in which the game ends as soon as one player reaches 100 points.

♠ ♦ ♣ ♥ ♠ ♦ ♣ ♥ ♠ ♦ ♣ ♥ ♠ ♦ ♣ ♥ ♠ ♦

Poker

♠ ♦ ♣ ♥

Poker has endless variants, but they fall into three main groups: Draw Poker, Stud Poker, and Texas Hold 'Em Poker.

Object: To win the pot, either by being the only player left or by having the best cards.

General Poker rules: These rules apply to all types of Poker games. In any individual game, it's important that all players know the bet limits and the rules. Here are the general rules of play:

Each player receives a stack or stacks of chips.

Deal and betting proceed clockwise (to the left).

At the showdown (end of the hand) the last to bet—or to raise the bet—shows first.

Players calling the final bet have a right to see the cards of all others who call.

If at any point only one player is left, that hand wins and need not be shown.

Once you've tried out several variations on the Poker theme, consider making up your own Poker game. Maybe your game will be the next rage!

Rank of hands in Poker: In descending order of rank, these are the hands of Poker.

Royal flush: Five sequential cards of the same suit to the ace (♥10-♥J-♥Q-♥K-♥A)

Straight flush: Any five sequential cards of the same suit (♥7-♥8-♥9-♥10-♥J)

The ♥ K is the high card. This player may check or bet. If ♥ K bets, then the player with the ♦ 10 sees the bet or else drops (by turning the ♦ 10 over), and so on with each player around the table. Since the ♥ K was the first king dealt, it has betting priority over the ♠ K.

Four of a kind: All four cards of a rank (♣6-♥6-♦6-♠6)

Full house: Three of a kind plus a pair (♥3-♠3-♣3-♦10-♠10)

Flush: Any five cards of a suit (♠Q-♠9-♠8-♠5-♠2)

♠ ♦ ♣ ♥ ♠ ♦ ♣ ♥ ♠ ♦ ♣ ♥ ♠ ♦ ♣ ♥ ♠ ♦

General terms in Poker:

Ante: Initial stake each player puts into the pot

Betting in the blind: Betting without seeing your cards

Bluffing: Betting or raising with a weak hand

Broadway: A straight to the ace

Call: To equal a bet made by another player

Check: To pass

Drop (or Fold): To quit a hand

(the) Goods: A real hand, no bluff

Hole cards: In Stud and Hold 'Em, face-down cards

Openers: A good enough card combination to meet a minimum requirement

Pat hand: A hand you don't draw to

Pot: All the bets in the center of the table

Pot limit: A dangerous game, where the bet limit is the sum of chips in the pot

Raise: To equal another's bet and add to it

Sandbag: To check (pass) and later raise in the same round

See a bet: To equal it; call

Sixth street: The last upcard in Seven-Card Stud, before a downcard is dealt

General terms in Poker: *(continued)*

Stand pat: Draw no cards

Trips: Three of a kind

Wheel: Ace through five for low

Wild cards: In some games, dealer may call certain cards wild, that is, they can stand for any other card. Sometimes a joker is added as a wild card. Deuces wild (all four of them) is another popular choice. Another favorite is One-eyes wild (the three face cards in profile: ♦K, ♥J, and ♠J).

Straight: Five cards in sequence, any suits. Ace can be either high or low (♦A-♥2-♣3-♦4-♠5).

Three of a kind: Three cards of one rank, the rest unmatched (♠K-♦K-♥K-♣9-♦7)

Two pair: Two different pairs of two cards of a rank, the fifth unmatched (♦J-♣J-♥8-♣8-♥5)

One pair: Two cards of a rank, the rest un-matched (♦J-♣J-♥8-♣7-♥5)

High card: No combination. Aces are high (♣A-♠7-♥9-♣10-♣4).

Between hands of the same type, the higher-ranked hand wins. For example, a flush headed by a jack (♣J-♣9-♣5-♣3-♣2) beats a flush to the 10 (♦10-♦9-♦8-♦5-♦3); queens up (♥Q-♦Q-♣3-♠3-♥4) beats 9s up (♠9-♥9-♣8-♥8-♠K).

Lowball Poker: Lowball Poker can be played in as many styles as high-only Poker. There is usually a

round of betting, a draw, then another betting round and a showdown. Aces rank low. The hand that ranks as the poorest Poker hand wins. For example, ♠7-♣3-♥9-♦4-♣5 (a 9-low) beats ♠4-♣A-♦2-♠J-♥3 (a jack-low).

Most lowball versions disregard flushes and straights and pay attention only to the number value of the cards, so that 7-6-5-4-3 is a 7-low. When hands competing for low have the same worst cards, look to the next worst card.

High-low Poker: In high-low Poker, the best hand and the worst hand divide the pot. Any form of Poker—Draw, Stud, or Hold 'Em—can be played high-low. High-low Poker has a few important differences from other games.

The declaration: In most split games, players declare, before the showdown, whether they are going high, low, or high and low. In some games, this is done out loud, by going around the table starting with the last raiser or bettor. This reduces some surprises and gives a certain positional advantage from which to play.

A more common practice is to declare silently, but at the same time. This can be done using chips or coins. At a signal, players either put no chips in their hand to go low, one chip in their hand to go high, or two chips to go high and low. In some games, this is the final action, after which the winners and losers are sorted out. In some games these declarations are followed by one more betting round (the drive) that gives bluffers and legitimate hands one more chance to raise the pot. Since one player may have a lock on

half the pot, high-low Poker limits raises to three per round.

Most high-low games encourage you to go for high and low on the same deal, if you've got the right hand. This is easy in seven-card games, where you can use different sets of cards for each direction you go. In five-card games, it must be clear whether a 2-3-4-5-6 straight can be low, that is, a 6-low. If you go high-low but lose in either direction (high or low), you win nothing.

♠ ♦ ♣ ♥

Draw Poker

♠ ♦ ♣ ♥

One of the best-known forms of the game, Draw Poker has been around for a long time and has fans worldwide.

Number of players: Two to seven

The cards: A regular pack of 52 cards is used.

To play: Each player antes one chip. Cards are dealt one by one until each player has five. The first player then may bet or check, but once a player has bet, each player in turn either folds or sees the bet (or perhaps raises it).

Once all bets and raises have been called, the dealer proceeds to ask each player in turn how many cards

they wish to draw. The maximum number of cards a player can draw is three. Each player casts unwanted cards aside, and the dealer deals replacements. Dealer's own draw should be clearly announced; for example, the dealer may state, "Dealer takes two." A player who draws no cards is said to stand pat.

Once players have all received their new cards, the final round of betting takes place, beginning with the player who made the last raise or bet. Most games establish a betting limit, which on the second round is usually double the first.

When all bets and raises have again been called, there is a showdown to see whose hand is best. Usually the last bettor shows first, and others may fold their hands if beaten. The remaining players have a right to see all hands that have called.

If all players pass on the first round, throw the hand in. The deal passes to the left, and another round of five cards is dealt. Leave the chips in the pot, as players add another ante.

Tips: Most fairly serious Poker games should have house rules that all players know in advance of play. For example, many games limit the number of raises in a round to three, unless only two players remain, who can then raise and re-raise each other as they wish. Other matters to clarify ahead of time include misdeals, misstatements of hands, maximum bets, and buying new chips, among other issues. To keep the Poker game friendly, take a few moments to make sure everyone is aware of the rules

♠ ♦ ♣ ♥ ♠ ♦ ♣ ♥ ♠ ♦ ♣ ♥ ♠ ♦ ♣ ♥ ♠ ♦

Stud Poker

♠ ♦ ♣ ♥

In Stud Poker, players see some of their opponents' cards, adding a new strategic element to the game.

Number of players: Two to eight

The cards: A regular pack of 52 cards is used.

To play: In Five-Card Stud Poker, each player antes. Deal one card down and one up to each player. Players look at their face-down cards.

The player with the highest card showing starts by checking or by betting. As soon as there's a bet, the players following must, in turn, either fold or call—or perhaps raise—the bet. Once all bets are called, the remaining players each receive another upcard. Another round of betting follows, started by the player with the best hand showing.

Each round of cards dealt up is followed by a betting round. The final round of bets occurs when all players left in the hand have four upcards. This round of betting should have a higher limit than the previous rounds. Also, if any player shows a pair at any time, the bet limit is raised.

After the final bets, the bettor—or last raiser—is usually first to turn over the hole card. If no one calls the last bet or raise, the winner gathers the pot and isn't obliged to show anyone the winning hand.

Variations: In Seven-Card Stud Poker, the mechanics work just as in Five-Card Stud Poker,

except that two hole cards are dealt before the first upcard. After a fourth upcard is dealt to each player, the next card is again dealt down, in the hole. After this, one more betting round ensues.

Any time a pair is showing, a higher bet limit applies. After the sixth and seventh cards, the higher bet limit also applies. To decide the pot, players use their best five cards out of the seven cards dealt.

♠ ♦ ♣ ♥

Texas Hold 'Em

♠ ♦ ♣ ♥

In the World Series of Poker, as well as smaller prize events, Texas Hold 'Em is the game they play.

Number of players: Two to twelve

Object: Best of any five cards from among the two in your hand and five on the board.

The cards: A regular pack of 52 cards is used.

To play: After each player antes, deal two cards face down to each player and five cards face down in the center of the table. Starting with the player at dealer's left, each player may check or bet. Once a player has made a bet, subsequent players must fold unless they see—or raise—the bet.

Once all first-round bets are called, the dealer turns over the first three face-down cards. These three cards

are called the flop. (The fourth is called the "turn" card; the fifth is the "river" card.)

Whoever was the last bettor starts a new round of betting, after which the dealer turns up one more card (turn) from the center of the table. Another betting round ensues, and then the dealer turns over the last card (river) for a final betting round. After all calls, the best hand wins the pot.

Tips: This is a game with no surefire advice, for each hand is different, and many different factors affect what the other players do. Some combinations, such as ♣K-♣Q, may seem to have greater prospects than ♦2-♠7, but if the flop is ♥7-♠2-♦7, you'd rather have the second hand.

♠ ♦ ♣ ♥

Anaconda

♠ ♦ ♣ ♥

Also known as Pass the Trash, this Poker game is popular played high-low.

Number of players: Three to seven

To play: Deal seven cards to each player. After a betting round, remaining players choose three cards to pass to the player on the left. Another betting round follows, and then players pass two cards to the left. Finally, after another betting round, players pass one

♠ ♦ ♣ ♥ ♠ ♦ ♣ ♥ ♠ ♦ ♣ ♥ ♠ ♦ ♣ ♥ ♠ ♦

card to their left. Now all players discard two cards, keeping five cards, which they place in order, face down.

There may now be a round of betting, or first, players may turn up (roll) one card. Thereafter, before each new round of betting, players roll one more card until each has only one card face down. Now the game looks just like Five-Card Stud Poker. After the declarations and final bets, players turn up their hidden card to reveal the winner(s).

Variations: To lower the number of betting rounds, in some games the three rounds of card passing precede any bets.

Another variant lets players keep all seven cards and choose the card to roll each round. This gives players chances to change directions during the roll. Before the final roll though, players must discard two cards and finish with five-card hands.

Different Anaconda passing procedures include having just one three-card pass or passing two cards to the left and one to the right.

Tips: Since you start out by reducing to four cards, to make a good hand you'll need help from the ones passed to you (unless you were dealt four of a kind). Because there are many rounds of betting, this is a risky game to run a bluff. It may work out, but you may run into a player with a strong hand, since the game offers several opportunities for hands to improve.

Also, try to remember the cards you pass and the cards you get passed. Occasionally, during the rolling phase, it may help you judge an opponent's unseen cards. For example, if your left-hand opponent rolls

A-2-3-4, but you have passed no card lower than a 10, you know this opponent can have a 10-low, at best.

♠ ♦ ♣ ♥

Chicago

♠ ♦ ♣ ♥

It's not certain whether this Poker game is played more often in Chicago than elsewhere, but it's exciting enough to be welcomed in any city.

Number of players: Three to seven

To play: Chicago is played like Seven-Card Stud High (see Stud Poker "Variations," p. 145), but the pot is divided between the high hand and whoever has the highest spade among their hole cards. The same player can win both halves of the pot. If no one has any spade in the hole, then the high hand wins the entire pot.

Tip: A player who bets heavily at every turn may have the ♠A in the hole, or perhaps may be betting heavily to build the pot for high hand or to discourage players who have a mid-range spade in the hole.

The more players seated at the table, the more likely that high spades are among the hole cards. Even facing six opponents, if you have the ♠K in the hole, the odds are still in your favor that the ♠A isn't among the 12 unseen cards. You'll be very pleased

seeing the ♠A appear as a turned card. The longer you don't, the greater the chance that it will be someone else's hole card!

Variations: Chicago has many variations. The lowest spade, not the highest, can take half the pot (count ace as high only). Or you might choose a payoff suit other than spades, just for a change. Another popular option is to let the lowest card in a player's hole, and all of the same rank, be wild for that player. Wild cards, of course, give everyone a chance for a high-ranking hand.

♠ ♦ ♣ ♥

Cincinnati

♠ ♦ ♣ ♥

Try the Iron Cross version of this Poker game for an interesting variation.

Number of players: Two to seven

To play: Deal each player five cards. Then deal five cards face down in the center. Before each round of betting, dealer turns over one card. In the showdown, use any combination of five cards from your hand and the common table cards.

Variation: For Iron Cross, deal the five cards in the form of a cross. In the showdown, you may combine

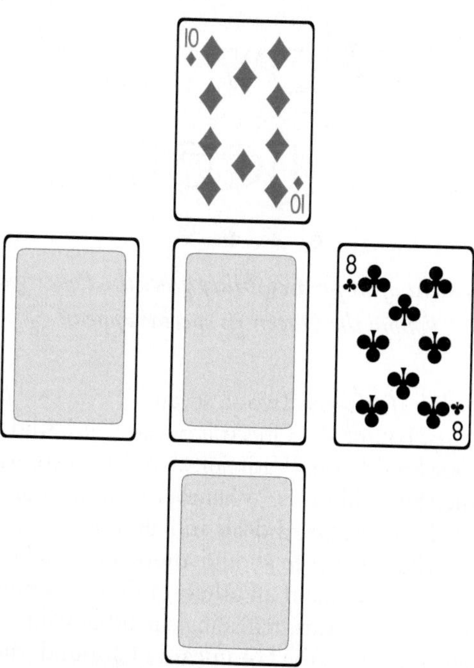

The first two cards revealed in Iron Cross should be from different arms of the cross. In some games, the center card, the last card turned up, is wild, along with any other cards of the same rank.

the cards in your hand with either arm (three cards in a line) of the Iron Cross.

♠ ♦ ♣ ♥

Follow the Queen

♠ ♦ ♣ ♥

An element of unpredictability gives the Poker game Follow the Queen its special appeal!

Number of Players: Two to seven

To play: Follow the Queen is Seven-Card Stud Poker (see Stud Poker "Variations," p. 145–146) with unpredictable wild cards. Whenever a queen is dealt as an upcard, the next card dealt and all others of its rank are wild. However, should another queen be dealt, the next card and all others of that rank now assume the wild status, replacing the other wild cards.

When a queen is the last upcard of a round, the first card dealt up in the next round and all others of the same rank are wild (until another queen turns up!). If the last upcard of the deal is a queen, then queens themselves are wild.

♠ ♦ ♣ ♥

♠ ♦ ♣ ♥ ♠ ♦ ♣ ♥ ♠ ♦ ♣ ♥ ♠ ♦ ♣ ♥ ♠ ♦

Omaha

♠ ♦ ♣ ♥

Can't get enough Hold 'Em? Here's a further expanded version of the popular Poker game.

Number of players: Three to eleven

To play: (See Texas Hold 'Em, p. 146.) Deal four cards to each player instead of two. In the showdown use two cards in your hand in combination with any three on the table. Often Omaha is played high-low, which can attract a lot of betting action.

Tip: With everyone holding four cards to the end, the caliber of winning hands rises. What you want, after the flop, is a clear winning hand so good that it's a lock—no one could have a better hand than yours. You want nothing to change this. But expect your hopes to be dashed occasionally in this game—the two cards you can't see may give someone else a better hand.

Here's an extreme case from high-low Omaha. You have ♣A-2-3, ♥A, and the flop is ♠A– 5, ♦A. This looks too good to be true: You have four aces for high, and for low you have 2-3, the best possible low cards. So, you bet. The next card, is the ♦J, and you bet some more.

But the last card turned is the ♠3! All of a sudden, you have only a jack-low! Probably everyone has better. In fact, another player looking at ♠4-2 has made not only a perfect 5-low (wheel) but also has a

lock on high—with a straight flush. After this hand, you'll be crying for a new deck, and for many weeks!

Variation: When played high-low, Omaha is one of several games where prevailing house rules can require that the low hand be an 8-low (e.g., 8-7-5-4-2) or better. If no one has an 8-low, the high hand takes the whole pot.

♠ ♦ ♣ ♥

Pineapple

♠ ♦ ♣ ♥

This one's another popular game in the Hold 'Em Poker family.

Number of players: Three to twelve.

To play: (See Texas Hold 'Em, p. 146.) Deal each player three cards and then five cards face down on the table. Before the flop, discard one card. In the showdown, use 0, 1, or 2 cards in your hand.

Variation: Crazy Pineapple is the same game, except the discard occurs after players see the three-card flop. In a variety known as Tahoe, players keep all three cards but must play exactly two. In some places, this is the game called Pineapple.

♠ ♦ ♣ ♥

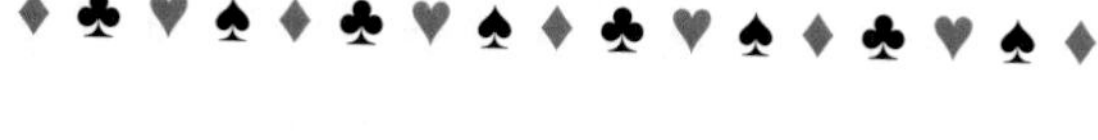

Razz

Razz is a lowball Poker game—the player with the worst five-card hand wins.

Number of players: Two to seven

To play: Deal and bet as in Seven-Card Stud high (see Stud Poker "Variations, " p. 145–146), with the maximum permitted bet raised with each round of betting. In some games, the rules may allow an increase in the betting limit on the third round if three cards to a 7-low show up for any player. The best possible hand is a 5-low.

Variations: Other forms of lowball poker, such as draw or Five-Card Stud, are also sometimes called Razz.

♠ ♦ ♣ ♥ ♠ ♦ ♣ ♥ ♠ ♦ ♣ ♥ ♠ ♦ ♣ ♥ ♠ ♦

Seven-Card No Peekie

♠ ♦ ♣ ♥

Here's a Poker game that has plenty of suspense.

Number of players: Two to seven

To play: All players ante an agreed amount. Deal seven cards to each player, kept face down, unseen.

The first player reveals three cards, and the first round of betting proceeds. The second player reveals as many cards as needed to beat the first player. (Example: If the first player turns ♥Q ♠7 ♣9, the second player will better that hand just by turning up a single ace or king.) The next round of betting follows.

Play and betting continues this way, with each player revealing as many cards as needed to beat the prior players, and if they cannot, they drop out of play. As it is unlikely that the first player's three cards will beat everyone else's seven cards, the first player will quite likely have a further opportunity to turn over more cards. High hand takes the pot.

Variations: In many games, the first player reveals only one card or two. More betting occurs with fewer revealed cards.

♠ ♦ ♣ ♥

♠ ♦ ♣ ♥ ♠ ♦ ♣ ♥ ♠ ♦ ♣ ♥ ♠ ♦ ♣ ♥ ♠ ♦

Star Wars

♠ ♦ ♣ ♥

Here's one more member of the popular Texas Hold 'Em Poker family.

Number of players: Three to eight
To play: Deal five cards to each player. Flop and betting are as in Texas Hold 'Em (p. 146), but you use two cards in your hand with three of the common cards. The difference from Texas Hold 'Em is subtle, but these games are distinct to serious Poker players.

♠ ♦ ♣ ♥

Super Hold 'Em

♠ ♦ ♣ ♥

Another Hold 'Em version for true lovers of the game.

Number of players: Three to eleven
To play: (See Texas Hold 'Em, p. 146.) Deal four cards to each player. Before the flop there's one discard, and after the flop there's another, both before betting. Use 0, 1, or 2 cards from your hand in combination with the cards on the table.
Tip: Super Hold 'Em encourages players to choose a hand to play without having to worry about calling

bets. Although you make your first discard in the blind (seeing only your own cards), you certainly want to give it thought. For example, hold on to two cards of the same suit to increase your chance of a flush.

At times, what you keep can be an outright guess. Say you are dealt ♣A-K, ♥A-K. You'll discard a king—praying that the flop has cards of the suit you kept no kings in and that you kept two cards in the right suit. Seeing the flop, which card to throw away might be clear, or again you might need to use your thinking cap. In Super Hold 'Em showdowns, players often have some pretty good cards, but not always!

♠ ♦ ♣ ♥

President

♠ ♦ ♣ ♥

Here's a game that's unimpeachable in every way!

Number of players: Three and up; the game is best with five or more.

Object: To be the first person to have no cards left in your hand (called president) and to avoid being the last with cards left in your hand (called the bum).

The cards: Use one regular pack of 52 cards. With six or more players, use a double deck.

To play: First dealer is chosen at random, but thereafter whoever is bum shuffles and deals. Cards

are all dealt out, making it likely that some players will receive one card more than the others.

Player to the left of dealer starts by playing a single card or a set of cards of the same rank. In turn, players may pass, play at least as many cards as the previous play but of higher rank, or play a larger set of cards of any rank. Your play must always be of the same rank.

A player who passes can play again on the same round, or trick, but any play that is followed by passes from all the other players ends that round. The trick

Here you see a sequence of plays in a five-player game. The ♠3 was led, followed by the ♦6, the ♥10, a pass, and two 2s. Then the leader passed, and the next player followed with a pair of 9s. The rest of the players passed, ending the trick. Note that each play was a set of cards higher than those in previous play.

is swept aside, and whoever played last starts the next round, again by playing any single card or set of cards of the same rank.

As players drop out of play by playing their last cards, those still left vie not to be bum.

At the end of play, players switch seats, if necessary. President gets the choice of most comfortable location, with vice president (see "Scoring") taking the next most comfortable chair, placed to president's left. Bum sits at president's right and deals so that for the next hand president plays first. For every deal following the first, before play bum gives president the highest card dealt to him or her, getting back from the president a card of president's choosing (usually a low one, of course).

Revolution: When a player plays four of a kind, rank order is inverted with aces becoming low and deuces high. The order of play is also reversed, going to the right instead of the left, until someone plays four of a kind again, as a counter-revolution. This can give the bum an opportunity to achieve a higher status. When playing with a double deck, the four of a kind must be all different suits.

Scoring: Whoever is first out of cards becomes president and scores 2 points. The next out of cards, vice president, scores 1 point. No one else gets a score. (Note: Scorekeeper should award the presidential and vice presidential points immediately.)

Tips: You can pass even when you have a legal move, and this can be good strategy. It pays to be a winner of a round, or trick, but it may help you to wait until later in the hand to be the last player to a

trick. At some point later you may gain the lead. This can let you play a series of cards that no one is in a position to beat: All pass and the cards are retired as you lead again.

Usually when leading to a trick you play single low cards, as they may not have any other convenient chance to be played. However, if it's your lead with ♠K ♦K ♥K ♦3 in your hand and another player will go out if you play the 3, play the kings first. If they are not bested, you win that trick and then play the 3: You are out of cards first!

Variations: In some games, president and bum have a two-card exchange. To save time, you might omit shifting seats. There are many play variations. In one, the first card played is always the ♣2. In another, playing a card or combination equal to those already played (e.g., two 9s following two other 9s) is a valid play.

In some circles, the deuce is considered the highest card, followed by ace, king, etc., down to 3 (lowest). Another variant is to include a joker, counting the joker on its own to be the highest possible group, which therefore ends any round of play.

Rummy

Rummy originated in the camps and saloons of the old West. As times changed, so did the game.

Number of players: Two to eight

Object: To score points for melds or to stop the game when you're ahead in points.

The cards: A regular pack of 52 cards is used.

To play: Deal ten cards to each player. Take turns taking cards from stock and making melds. Players try to be first to go out or to stop play (knock) while they have more points.

Melds in all Rummy games: Melds in Rummy consist of groups of three or more cards of the same rank or sequences of three or more cards in one suit.

♠ ♦ ♣ ♥

Gin Rummy

♠ ♦ ♣ ♥

Back in the 1930s, Gin was a minor branch of the Rummy family tree when suddenly Hollywood stars embraced it. Gin Rummy quickly became a national craze.

Number of players: Two or three; or four can play as partners.

Object: To meld your cards and score for Gin.

The cards: A regular pack of 52 cards is used. Aces are low.

To play: Deal ten cards to each player. Turn one card up—the knock card—to begin a discard pile, placing the remaining cards face down next to it as a draw pile.

Nondealer may take the knock card and discard. If nondealer declines the knock card, dealer may take it and discard. Should neither player want the knock card, nondealer draws the top card from stock and discards.

Turns alternate. At each play, take either the top discard or the top card from stock and then discard. Look to match cards in your hand into melds. When all your cards are melded, call "Gin" (or "Gin Rummy"), discard face down, and show your hand.

Knocking: If you wish to stop the round before you or your opponent reaches gin, you may knock. Simply

discard face down and say, "Knock." Or, just rap the table. Put down, or table, your melds, setting aside your unmatched cards—called deadwood. Your total deadwood count must not be greater than the original knock card (see "Scoring" for card values). If you have ♣10-♣J-♣Q-♣K, ♠9-♣9-♥9, ♦A, ♠2, ♣4, your deadwood cards offer little melding hope. Since their count totals only 7, if the knock card is 8 or higher, you should knock.

In the example shown, the player with the top hand went rummy. The unmelded cards in the loser's hand, ♦J, ♦9, ♣9, and ♣8, yielded 36 points to the winner.

Laying off: After a player knocks, opponent has the opportunity to lay off any possible melds onto the tabled melds. In this way, opponent can reduce his or her point total (see "Scoring"). Laying off is not permitted after a Gin.

Scoring: Unmelded picture cards count 10, and all others their face value (aces count 1). If you Gin, score your opponent's deadwood total, plus a 25-point bonus. If you knock, score the difference between your knock count and opponent's remaining deadwood cards after opponent has the opportunity to make layoffs.

As sometimes happens—especially after laying off—your knock count may be greater than your opponent's deadwood. In this case, opponent scores the difference in count, plus a 20-point bonus for the underknock (also called undercut). If your opponent lays off every unmelded card, the bonus is 25 points for ginning off.

Should neither player make Gin or knock, the hand is thrown in. Common practice is to stop play when two cards are still left in the draw pile. Game is generally played to 100 points.

Tips: Gin is a good game for memory training: It will pay to recall which cards have already been played, especially the ones taken by your opponent. Be aware, however, that your opponent will also notice the discards you pick up!

A few helpful don'ts:

• Don't pick up a discard unless it gives you a meld or unless you have a very poor hand and your pick opens up a few chances. An exception might be to pick up a

low-count discard (an ace or deuce) when you have a bad hand and a safe discard to make.

•Don't hold on to a high melding chance that only one card can fill. For instance, don't hold on to ♦10-♦Q if you can draw any better or lower cards.

• Don't expect to find a third ace when you have two unless you get lucky and draw it from the draw pile. That's not a card your opponent would discard except with a very good hand.

• Don't play for Gin when you can knock early.

Variations: When the upcard turned is an ace, it's a common practice to play the hand for Gin—knocking isn't allowed. In many games, you count the hand double if the upcard is a spade. Another custom is for nondealer to receive an eleventh card, with no upcard turned. Play begins with nondealer's discard. You may knock any time your deadwood count is 10 or less.

In Three-Handed Gin Rummy, it's more difficult to reach a Gin hand, unless you allow both opponents a shot at the discard.

500 Rummy

♠ ♦ ♣ ♥

This topsy-turvy form of Rummy has also been called Pinochle Rum and Michigan Rum.

Number of players: Two to eight, but the game works best with three to five.

Object: To score points for melds and to meld all your cards.

The cards: For two to four players, a regular pack of 52 cards is used. For five or more players, use two packs of 52 cards. Aces are high or low.

To play: For two players, deal ten cards each; for more players, deal seven cards each. Melds score according to the cards they contain: High aces count 15, low aces 1, face cards 10, all others their face value.

The use of the discard pile is common. In other Rummy games, the discard pile is a tight stack, with only its top card in view. Here, the discard pile is spread out so that all cards are in view.

Play starts at dealer's left, and at your turn you may take the top card from stock, or you can take any card in the discard pile—not just the top discard—as long as you use it as part of a meld. You also have to take all cards above the discard you take. This is helpful, since your goal is to meld many points.

When you make a meld, you lay it on the table rather than keeping it in your hand. On subsequent

turns, besides making melds, you can also lay cards off on your own or others' melds (that is, add cards to them). Since you'll be tallying your melds at the end of the hand, keep layoffs on others' melds within your own melding area.

The game ends when any player goes out—melds or lays off every card, with or without a final discard. No further melds, plays, or discards may occur. If no player should go out, the game ends when the entire stock is exhausted.

Scoring: At the end of play, total your melded cards, then subtract the count of cards left in your hand (whether meldable or not). Record each player's score. There is no added bonus for going out.

Tips: The strategy of 500 Rummy is nearly the opposite of other Rummy games. Keep high cards longer, because they're worth more. Since a discard can be available later, you may break up a low-scoring meld, allowing you to pick up more cards later. Be careful: Someone else may have the same idea, and you could lose your card!

♠ ♦ ♣ ♥

♠ ♦ ♣ ♥ ♠ ♦ ♣ ♥ ♠ ♦ ♣ ♥ ♠ ♦ ♣ ♥ ♠ ♦

Knock Rummy

♠ ♦ ♣ ♥

Knowing when to knock is the key to winning this member of the Rummy family.

Number of players: Two to five is best, but six may play.

Object: To knock when you have a lower deadwood count than any of your opponents.

The cards: A regular pack of 52 cards is used. Aces are low.

To play: For two players, deal ten cards each. For three or four players, deal seven cards each. With five or six players, deal just six cards each, leaving enough cards for each player to have several turns.

Knock Rummy proceeds like Gin Rummy, with two major differences. The first difference is that you may knock on any turn, with any deadwood count, and the second is that no cards are laid off on the knocker's melds. As the play rotates, the discard is available only to the player whose turn it currently is.

Scoring: When someone knocks, show your cards, separating melded combinations from deadwood. Whoever has the lowest deadwood count wins the difference from each other player. If you knock and are tied, the player you tie with is deemed the winner and collects from the others. When you knock and find that you do not have the lowest hand, pay an extra 10 points to the winner of the hand.

When you knock with a fully melded hand (going rummy), you win a 25-point bonus from each player, in addition to their deadwood counts.

Tips: With two players, if you're dealt a deadwood count in the 40s, that may often be lower than your opponent's count. Since losing costs an additional 10-point penalty, however, you should probably make a quick knock only if under 35.

With more players, the added bonus for going rummy may influence you to play out a hand with an early meld. That's okay if your deadwood cards are relatively high (7s and above) or if your unmelded cards have a good chance of making a meld. But if your deadwood count is low, you should end the round as early as possible—before your opponents draw enough lucky cards to win.

♠ ♦ ♣ ♥

Oklahoma

♠ ♦ ♣ ♥

Here's a Rummy game that shares several features of Canasta!

Number of players: Two to five, but the game is best when played by three or four.

Object: To score 1,000 points by melding sets and sequences.

The cards: Two complete decks plus one joker, 105 cards in all. The joker and all eight deuces are wild and may stand for any card.

To play: Deal 13 cards to each player. Place the remaining cards face down as a draw pile, turning up the top card to start a discard pile. Players each in turn have the opportunity to pick up the first upcard by melding it with at least two cards in their hand. Whoever does this then discards, and play then proceeds to the next player to the left. You may discard a ♠Q only if you have no other discard.

If no one takes the upcard, then the player at dealer's left starts by drawing a card, tabling any melds, and discarding. At your turn, you may also add, or lay off, a card to one of your existing melds. Play continues clockwise, and the top discard is available only to the player whose turn it is. If you pick up the discard, you must meld it immediately or lay it off on one of your existing melds. Picking up the discard also means taking all cards beneath it as well, and any cards so taken may be melded on the same turn before discarding, or on a later turn. All melds remain on the table.

In a meld, if the card a wild card represents isn't clear, then specify it exactly. For example, in ♥8-♠2-♥10 it's obvious that ♠2 stands for the ♥9, but in ♥8-♥9-♠2, the player making the meld should specifically say whether the wild card represents the ♥10 or ♥7, as either is possible. If the meld is ♥8-♠2-♣2, the melder must state whether the meld is a set of 8s or a sequence in hearts.

You can replace the joker with the card it stands for in a meld, take it back in your hand, and use it

A hand of Oklahoma in progress, with melds of two players already on the table.

again later. You cannot replace a melded deuce.

When a player goes out (discards and has no cards left), the hand is over.

Melds: Oklahoma has two kinds of valid melds:

1) Sets: three or four of the same rank, e.g., ♥J-♣J-♣J or ♣6-♦2-♠6-♥6.

2) Sequences: three or more consecutive cards in the same suit, e.g., ♦9-10-J. Ace can rank either high or low (A-K-Q or 3-2-A), but a sequence cannot round the corner—2-A-K is not permitted.

Laying off: You can add one or more cards to your own melds. A set is limited to four cards. A sequence, however, can be up to 14 cards, one ace being low and the other high.

Scoring: When the hand ends, cards melded count for you, while those left in your hand count against

you. Aces are worth 20, 8s and higher (except the ♠Q) count 10; 7s and lower count 5. A deuce in a meld is worth the card it represents, but a deuce in the hand is penalized 20 points. In a meld, the ♠Q counts 50, but it costs 100 in the hand. Melded, the joker counts 100, but it receives a 200-point penalty if caught in a player's hand. A player who goes out earns a bonus of 100 points. Going out concealed (without having made a prior meld) earns an additional bonus of 250, but these points do not count toward the points needed for game. Game goes to 1,000 points.

Tips: You should try to keep a high ♠ or a queen in your hand in order to be able to meld more easily any ♠Q you might draw. Also, when you have a set of four to meld, consider melding just three of them. Hold on to the fourth card to possibly use in a different meld. Unless someone goes out, you can add it later to the melded set.

Variation: In some games, when you add cards to a sequence meld that contains a wild card, you can change the wild card's identity. For example, you may add ♥10 to ♥8-♥9-♠2, and now declare the ♠2 to be either the ♥7 or ♥J.

♠ ♦ ♣ ♥ ♠ ♦ ♣ ♥ ♠ ♦ ♣ ♥ ♠ ♦ ♣ ♥ ♠ ♦

Schafkopf

♠ ♦ ♣ ♥

Also spelled Schafskopf, this game of strategy emphasizes skill in taking tricks. In the United States, it's often known by its translated name, Sheepshead.

Number of players: Three (Four or five players may sit at the table, with players taking turns sitting out.)

Object: To win at least 61 of 120 points available in tricks.

The cards: A 32-card pack, formed by omitting all 2s through 6s, is used. All queens, jacks, and diamonds are trumps. The plain suits—spades, clubs, and hearts—rank A (high)-10-K-9-8-7. The rank of the trumps is ♣Q-♠Q-♥Q-♦Q-♣J-♠J-♥J-♦J-♦A-♦10-♦K-♦9-♦8-♦7.

To play: The three players are called forehand (to dealer's left), middlehand, and endhand. Deal one round of three cards each, then two face-down cards—called the skat—that are set aside, a round of four cards, and another round of three cards, for a total of ten cards per player.

First, determine who will become the player against the other two. Starting with forehand, either accept the role of player by picking up the skat and discarding two cards, or pass. If no one accepts, play the deal as a "least" (see "Scoring").

No matter who is player, forehand starts play by leading any card to the first trick. Always follow suit

Card Counts:	
Ace	11 points
Ten	10 points
King	4 points
Queen	3 points
Jack	2 points
7, 8, and 9	0 points

Each player gains or loses game points as follows, based on points in play:

Points in play	*Game points*
61–90	2
91+ (Schneider)	4
winning all tricks (Schwarz)	6
31–60	– 2
0–30	– 4
winning no tricks	– 6

when able, but otherwise play any card. A trick is won by the highest trump in it, or, lacking any trumps, by the highest card of the suit led. Whoever wins a trick leads to the next until all ten tricks have been taken.

Scoring: At the end of play, each side counts points taken in tricks. Player must win at least 61 of the 120 points in play (including the two discards in the count).

This hand is quite good. You have six trumps, including the two highest. You haven't seen the skat yet, but you can plan to salt away the two 10s, which will count 20 points in your trick total later.

Player's two opponents work together to win points and defeat the player. Their chief strategy is to add high-scoring cards to each other's tricks.

When the hand is played at "least," everyone tries to take as few points as possible. Whoever has the lowest total wins 2 game points, and a player taking no tricks scores 6 game points. If two players tie for least, whoever did not take the most recent trick (between the two) wins the 2 game points. If all three players tie at 40 points each, endhand scores the 2 game points. If you take all the tricks, you lose 4 game points. The game ends when someone scores 10 game points.

Tips: To accept the role of player, you almost certainly need more than your one-third share of the 14 trumps. And since you'll need to score points, it helps to have an ace or two.

Of the 120 points, 75 come from the aces, 10s, and kings of the plain suits, which have only six cards each. You can't count on everyone following even to the first lead. In fact, the player's two discards often create a void in at least one plain suit. When defending, one way to win an ace is to play it when your co-defender is winning a trick in another suit. Especially when you have very few trumps, look for chances to smear—to discard an ace or 10—on your side's trick.

♠ ♦ ♣ ♥

Sixty-Six

Sixty-Six is a quiet game with good interplay. The name comes from the scoring: since 130 points are in the game, you need more than half—you need 66 points to win the hand.

Number of players: Two

Object: To score 66 points by trick-taking and melding K-Q marriages.

The cards: A 24-card deck of 9s through aces is used. In every suit, cards rank A-10-K-Q-J-9.

To play: Deal six cards to each player, three at a time. Turn up one card designating trumps; place it slightly under the rest of the pack.

Scoring:	
Marriage in trumps	40
Marriage in another suit	20
Each ace taken in a trick	11
Each 10 taken in a trick	10
Each king taken in a trick	4
Each queen taken in a trick	3
Each jack taken in a trick	2

To begin the first phase of play, nondealer leads any card and dealer plays any card. You needn't follow suit, and you may trump opponent's lead.

Each trick is won by the higher trump or else by the high card of the suit led. After each trick, both players take a new card from the stock. The winner of the trick draws first and leads to the next one.

Whoever has the 9 of trumps may exchange it for the trump upcard, as long as that player has won at least one trick. However, if the 9 of trumps is the last card drawn from stock, it's not exchanged; the other player takes the upcard.

Play continues in this way until the cards have all been drawn. When only two draw cards are left, the loser of that trick takes the trump upcard.

When the stock is gone, players continue to play tricks from their hands but must follow suit; they may trump or play any card if unable to follow suit.

Marriages: A marriage consists of the king and queen of the same suit (see "Scoring"). To claim a

marriage on your turn, show it and then lead one of the cards.

Closing: Before the stock is gone, a player having the lead may announce, "The game is closed." The player then turns over the trump upcard. No more cards are drawn and the play advances to phase two. Marriages may still be declared.

Taking the last trick scores 10 unless either player closed the game. A player reaching 66 or more scores 1 game point if opponent has 34 or more, 2 game points if opponent has 33 or less, and 3 game points should opponent have no tricks at all. The first player to score 7 game points is the winner.

During play, a player can announce 66, terminating play. The remaining cards are not played or scored. If the player announcing 66 doesn't actually have 66, opponent scores 2 game points. Should the final tally show both players over 66, but with neither having announced it, neither scores.

Tips: Keep track of your points so you can predict when you will hit 66. If you have the trump marriage, worth 40, you need only 26 other points. If all you need to win is a few tricks, close the game. If you have high nontrump cards, you may want to close the game just to protect a good trick-taking hand.

♠ ♦ ♣ ♥ ♠ ♦ ♣ ♥ ♠ ♦ ♣ ♥ ♠ ♦ ♣ ♥ ♠ ♦

Solo

♠ ♦ ♣ ♥

This popular trick-taking game—a cousin of Whist—gives players a chance to form occasional temporary partnerships.

Number of players: Four

Object: To win enough tricks to fulfill your contract.

The cards: A regular pack of 52 cards is used. Aces are high.

To play: The turn to deal passes clockwise. Deal 13 cards to each player, turning dealer's last card up to specify a trump suit. The player at dealer's left, eldest hand, acts first. Eldest hand may pass or make one of the following calls, listed in rank from low to high:

Proposal (Prop): To take eight of 13 tricks with another player as partner.

Solo: To take five of 13 tricks playing alone against the three other players.

Misère (mee-ZAIR): To take no tricks, playing alone with no suit as trumps.

Abondance (Abundance): To take nine of 13 tricks, playing alone against three opponents, with a suit other than the upcard as trumps. When this is the final call, announce the trump suit before the opening lead is made.

Misère Ouverte (mee-ZAIR oo-VAIRT): To take no tricks, with no suit as trumps, and with the hand exposed on the table (also called Spread).

Abondance in Trumps (Royal Abondance): To take nine of 13 tricks, with the upcard suit as trumps.

Abondance Declared: To take all 13 tricks against the other players, naming a suit as trumps.

You may only make a call if it outranks a prior call. For example, if a player has called Misère, you cannot then call Prop or Solo.

Prop and cop: You propose by saying "I propose." Any player who has not passed may accept (cop) the proposal, agreeing to play the hand as the proposer's partner, as long as no higher call has been made. If you "prop" and no one accepts, you may convert your call into a higher one or else throw the hand in.

Scoring:

Each deal of Solo is scored independently. You may collect, or pay off, according to this typical scoring scale:

Proposal	5 points
Solo	10 points
Misère	20 points
Abondance	30 points
Misère Ouverte	30 points
Abondance in Trump	40 points
Abondance Declared	60 points

Hearts are trumps. Even though West's ♥s themselves are weak, the hand as a whole is well-suited to prop. In this case, North would immediately cop, and that would likely be the final call. (East might try Misère but is likely to be forced to win a trick in clubs.) At ♥s, West and North together would probably win 9 of 13 tricks. If West were to pass and not prop, then North will certainly prop, and before West gets a chance to accept, South will cop. As partners, North and South will likely take 9 or 10 tricks.

A player who passes cannot later make a call, with the exception of the eldest player, who may accept a proposal after passing.

Regardless of who makes the final call, eldest hand leads to the first trick. The exception is at Abondance Declared, when the caller leads first. Dealer should remember to pick up the upcard before the second trick.

Players follow suit whenever possible, but otherwise may play any card. A trick is won by the highest trump it contains or by the highest card of the suit led when it contains no trump. The winner of each trick leads to the next.

Tips: Hands scoring more than Misère don't come up that often, but they are quite recognizable when you do come across one of them. An Abondance hand might be ♣A-♣K-♣J-♣10-♣9-♣6-♦A-♦K-♦10-♦5-♦4-♠5-♥7. A Misère Ouverte could be ♣A-♣10-♣6-♣5-♣3-♣2-♦J-♦7-♦4-♦3-♦2-♠4-♥3.

Variation: When all players pass, the hand is usually thrown in, but you may instead play a grand, a no-trump contract where the winner of the final trick loses 10 points to each other player.

Spades

It's curious that not much has been written about this widely known, easy-to-learn game. It's gathering new devotees from urban America, on college campuses, and even in cyberspace!

Number of players: Four, playing as partners

Object: To win at least the number of tricks bid by your side.

The cards: A regular pack of 52 cards is used. Aces are high.

To play: Partners sit opposite each other. Dealer deals 13 cards to each player. Spades are always trumps. There's one round of bidding, which starts at dealer's left. The first two players both bid the number of tricks—or books—they expect to take, while the second player in each partnership bids the total for the pair. For example, you deal, the player on your left bids four, your partner bids three, the next player bids five, and you bid seven. Your side has bid for seven tricks, and your opponents have bid for five tricks.

There are several special bids that are optional in Spades.

10 for two: A contract for ten books without a partner, with a two-to-one payoff.

Nil: A bid by the first bidder for a side for no tricks, which partner must convert to four tricks.

Blind nil: Similar to nil except the player may not look at the cards beforehand, though before play you and your partner may exchange one card. Your side must be down by 200 points to go for a bid of blind nil.

The player at dealer's left may lead any card other than a spade to the first trick. You must follow suit if able, otherwise play any card. A trick is won by the highest spade it contains or, if it contains no spade, by the highest card of the suit led.

The winner of each trick leads to the next. Until a spade has been played on a nonspade lead, you can't lead spades unless all you have in your hand are spades. When you win a book, gather it in a packet that everyone can count.

Scoring: If your side makes its bid, score the bid number times 10, plus 1 for each extra trick, called a

If you are dealt many spades and some other high cards, bid 10 for two on your own. Any high spades or diamonds your partner might have are helpful to your side whether they are in play or not!

sandbag. If your side fails to make at least the amount bid, you lose ten times the number of tricks bid. For example, your side bids seven, and your opponents bid five. You make nine tricks, while your opponents make four. Your side scores 72 points (7 × 10, plus two sandbags); opponents lose 50 (their bid, times 10).

If you succeed at 10 for two, you win 200 points, but if you fail, you lose 100. For nil, you win 100 or lose 100 as the case may be, but for blind nil you win 200 at the risk of 100.

Sandbags: When your sandbags total ten, subtract 100 points from your score (don't add 10). This works as a slow penalty for underbidding the number of books you take. Any leftover sandbags start a new count to ten.

Play until one side reaches 500 points.

Tips: Because of sandbags, winning extra books is no help, so be on the lookout for a situation where you have both the high card and the low card in a suit and can control winning a book or losing it. If you have ♠10-♠7, for example, and you know that the only spade remaining is an opponent's ♠8, depending upon the number of tricks you want, you can choose whether to win the ♠8 or lose it.

Variations: In some games, the ♦2 is used as an extra trump, ranking between the ace and king. Some games add a joker for an extra trump and leave out a plain-suit deuce. An interesting alternative to start the hand is for all players to put out their lowest club (or lowest diamond, lacking clubs) for the first book. The high club in this book wins it and leads to the next trick. With the first book played this way, the strate-

gies for bidding and play are a little different.

Some Spades games allow a generous amount of informal chat between partners before deciding on their bid. You can say nearly anything except what cards you hold.

♠ ♦ ♣ ♥

Spite and Malice

♠ ♦ ♣ ♥

Spite and Malice gives plenty of chances for planning, strategy, and surprise. It won't take you long to appreciate the game's whimsical name.

Number of players: Two

Object: To play off all your payoff pile cards, or at least more of them than your opponent can.

The cards: Two 52-card decks plus their four jokers are used. Kings are high and aces are low.

To play: The two players sit across from each other. Shuffle all four jokers with one of the decks; this creates a shared draw pile. Shuffle and divide the other deck equally so that each player has a face-down 26-card payoff pile.

Each player turns up the top card of their payoff pile, and whoever shows the lower card deals a five-card hand from the draw pile to each player. Non-dealer plays first.

At each turn you must play any aces you have—in hand or on your payoff pile—to the center of the table. These aces start the center stacks.

In your turn, you may make any, all, or none of the other possible plays. You can play a card from your hand to begin one of four side stacks (start one side stack per turn, until you have four). You can play one or more cards from your hand onto one or more of your own side stacks. Each card added must either be the same rank as the top card on the pile or else be one rank lower (any 5 on any 6). You can move the top card from a side stack, either onto another side stack or to start a new side stack. You can play a card from your hand, your payoff pile, or your side stacks onto the center stacks. You play a 2 on an ace, a 3 on a 2, a 4 on a 3, and so forth, upward to the king. Suit does not matter.

Before beginning your turn, draw cards from the draw pile to replace cards you've played, maintaining your hand at five cards. Keep playing until you cannot make a further play or choose not to do so. When a center stack is built up to the king, shuffle all 13 cards in with the remaining draw cards.

Jokers: A joker can stand for any card except an ace. You can play jokers onto the shared center piles or onto your own side stacks.

Bonus turns: Whenever you play all five cards from your hand at once, you get an extra turn. Take five new cards from the draw pile and keep playing.

♠ ♦ ♣ ♥ ♠ ♦ ♣ ♥ ♠ ♦ ♣ ♥ ♠ ♦ ♣ ♥ ♠ ♦

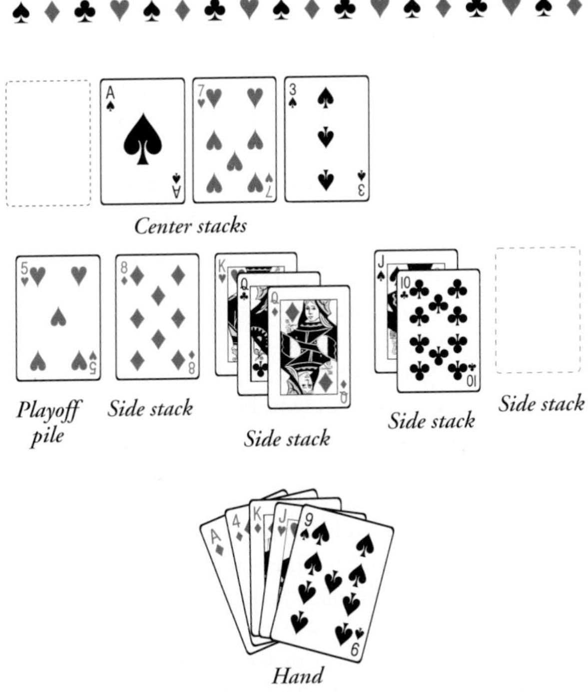

You must play the ♦ A from your hand to start a new center pile. You can follow by playing the ♦ 4 from your hand and ♥ 5 from your payoff pile onto the ♠ 3, turning over the new payoff pile card. You can then continue further, building the ♥ 7 up to king by using the remaining cards in your hand with the 8, 10, and Q in your side stacks. This lets you draw 5 new cards, and it's still your turn.

If neither player can—or will—make a play, the game is blocked. In a blocked game, you must make any obvious plays that opponent requests.

Scoring: A player who goes out (plays off the whole payoff pile) scores the number of cards left in opponent's payoff pile plus a 10-point bonus. In a blocked game, whoever has fewer payoff-pile cards scores the difference, with no bonus. Play to 25 points or to any other agreed-upon number.

Tips: Your immediate goal is always to try to play off your top payoff-pile card. It's well worth spending a joker or two to get to it.

A constant goal is to make things difficult for your opponent. For example, try to build center stacks just past the rank of the payoff-pile card your opponent currently has showing.

Try to start your side stacks with high cards, giving yourself more room to build downward. You can play cards of the same rank to side stacks, but it becomes harder to empty such piles. Sequential piles play right off onto center stacks.

Variations: Some versions let you play only one card in any turn to a side stack. Others follow the rule that layoffs in sequence must alternate between red and black cards. In some games, players do not take a bonus turn for playing out all five cards from the hand—or else the bonus is allowed only if all five cards play into the center. You can play a blocked game out to the end by collecting all cards except for those still in the payoff piles. Shuffle this whole bundle together, deal five cards to each player, and resume the game.

♠ ♦ ♣ ♥

Twenty-One

♠ ♦ ♣ ♥

Don't confuse this game with the casino game of Blackjack, also called 21. Even children can play this easy-to-learn numbers game, and anyone can win!

Number of players: Two to seven

Object: To win as many cards as possible without going over 21.

The cards: A regular pack of 52 cards is used. Aces and picture cards count 1 point each, all others count their face value.

To play: Deal the cards out equally, and set aside any remaining cards. Starting at dealer's left and continuing clockwise around the table, players build a card count up to 21. As each card is played, the new total is announced.

When you play a card that reaches 21 exactly, collect the cards in the center. However, when any card you have would go over 21, say "Stop." The player on your right collects the cards. The player who said "Stop," begins the next count toward 21. The hand is over when the final player gathers in the last cards.

Scoring: Players count the cards they've won, each card counting 1 point. The first player to 50 points (or any other agreed-upon total) wins.

Tip: A usual strategy for most players is to play their high-count cards early. This leads to more low

The count has gone 6-14-15-19. If you have a 2, you can score 21 exactly and win the cards. If you have an ace or a picture card, you can still play. Otherwise, say, "Stop." The player on your right gathers in the cards, and you begin a new count.

cards in the later rounds, and so the center pile tends to be bigger after the first few build to 21.

Variations: You can play this game blind, with each player turning up a card from a pile at each turn without knowing its value.

A similar game called Twenty-Nine is intended for partnership play. Deal 13 cards to each player. The player at dealer's left begins by playing any card, and players follow in turn, stating the new total with each card played. If you can't play without going past 29, you must pass. Whoever reaches 29 exactly wins the trick. The next player then lays down a card to begin a new count. Eight tricks are possible, although they are not always taken in play. The side with the most cards when no one can play exactly to 29 wins.

♠ ♦ ♣ ♥

♠ ♦ ♣ ♥ ♠ ♦ ♣ ♥ ♠ ♦ ♣ ♥ ♠ ♦ ♣ ♥ ♠ ♦

2-10-Jack

♠ ♦ ♣ ♥

This game is quick and nifty with lots of little agonies and ironies. In pursuing the high-scoring cards, you might instead wind up taking high negative-scoring cards.

Number of players: Two

Object: To win tricks containing plus cards and to lose tricks containing minus cards.

The cards: A regular pack of 52 cards is used. Hearts are always trumps; aces are high. The ♠A is called Speculation. It outranks all the other cards including the ♥A when used as trump.

To play: Deal six cards each, one at a time, and place the remaining cards face down as a stock pile.

Nondealer leads to the first trick. You must follow suit if able; otherwise you must trump. If you have no trump, play any card. If a trick contains no trump, it is won by the higher card of the suit that is led.

If a trump is led, the player holding Speculation has the option of playing it as the highest trump but is not forced to play Speculation when it's the only possible trump. You may also use it to trump a club or diamond trick, and you must do so if it's your only trump. You must play Speculation on a spade lead if it's your only spade. When leading Speculation, state whether it's a spade or a trump.

You could start with ♠ 2, which opponent, holding any spade or any trump, must take. If you can guess that opponent has no spades, lead ♠ A (Speculation) as a ♠, forcing opponent to capture it by trumping. You'd like to be able to win with the ♥ J—if you lead it early in the game, opponent is less likely to be holding the ♥ A, ♥ K, or ♥ Q, which could capture it.

After each trick, both players take a new card from the stock, the winner of the trick drawing first. The winner of each trick leads to the next. Continue until all tricks have been taken.

Scoring: Sort the scoring cards in your tricks (see table on the next page). Add up the plus cards, subtract the minus cards, and enter your scores accordingly. The players' combined scores must be +5, and it's easy to see why—the hearts and spades cancel each other out, leaving five cards of +1. The winner is the first player to get to +31.

Count of cards:	
♥2, ♥10, ♥J	+10 each
♥A, ♥K, ♥Q	+ 5 each
♠2, ♠10, ♠J	−10 each
♠A, ♠K, ♠Q	−5 each
♣A, ♣K, ♣Q, ♣J	+ 1 each
♦6	+ 1

Tips: 2-10-Jack is not an easy game to control. You have only six cards at once, and you don't know whether you'll be getting useful cards or dangerous cards from the stock. As in many games, recalling the cards already played helps a lot, and so does counting trumps. The 3 through 9 of trumps can be good or bad to have. They can protect your other hearts, but they could wind up trumping high minus cards in spades.

Along with Old Maid, War is one of the first card games we played as children. In practical terms, it rarely ends with a complete defeat.

Number of players: Two or more
Object: To win all the cards.
The cards: A regular pack of 52 cards is used. Aces are high.

To play: Divide the pack equally into a face-down pile for each player. At about the same time, each player turns over their top card. Whoever has the higher card wins both cards, and the process is repeated. Cards won may be placed on the bottom

When there is a tie for high card, a war is waged to determine the winner. Here, players were tied at 5, and the player with the ♥ K is the winner of this war.

of your pack or set aside until your pile runs down, at which point the cards taken must be played.

Occasionally, both players turn up cards of the same rank. This starts a war, in which each player lays off three more cards face down and then turns up the next card. Whoever's card is higher wins all the cards from that war. If the new upcards are also tied, turn three more cards face down and then turn the next card up to determine the winner of the war.

The game ends when one player has taken all the cards, but this can take a long time. You can try a shorter game, where you go through the cards just once or twice, and then see who has more cards. You may also decide to play until one player's hand is reduced to ten cards.

Variation: For three or more players, deal the cards out as equally as possible. Turn cards as before, and when players tie for best card, each plays two more face-down cards, with the next card turned up to decide a winner. Players not in the war must also contribute their next three cards. Play continues until one player has all the cards.

Whist

♠ ♦ ♣ ♥

Some might consider this ancestor of Bridge and other games to be obsolete. Nonetheless, even today Whist offers a nice combination of luck, skill, and surprise.

Number of players: Four, in pairs with partners facing each other.

Object: To win a majority of the 13 tricks.

The cards: A regular deck of 52 cards is used. By custom, dealer's partner shuffles a second deck for the other side to use on the following hand.

To play: Deal 13 cards to each player, with the last card dealt face up to designate the trump suit. Player at dealer's left leads any card, and dealer, before playing to the first trick, picks up the turned-up card. Whenever possible, players follow suit but otherwise may play any card, including a trump. A trick is won by the highest trump card in it or else by the highest card played of the suit led. The winner of each trick leads to the next trick.

Score: The side taking the majority of tricks scores 1 point for each trick won over six. For example, a side that wins 10 of 13 tricks scores 4. Game goes to the first side to reach 10 points or any other agreed-upon number.

Tips: In order to win the majority of tricks, you must do more than take tricks with aces—you must try to make winners out of lower cards. For example,

♦s are trump and your hand includes ♣Q-J-10. Even when the opponents have both ♣A and ♣K, if you can lead ♣ twice, you establish a high card in the suit. Even if your ♣s are Q-9-6-4, lead the ♣4, and see what happens. If partner has some high clubs, you may together be able to make the ♣Q high to win a trick later.

In general, at the start of play, when you are long in trumps (4 or more cards), lead another long suit if you have one. When you have a short trump holding (2 or fewer), lead another short suit.

♠ ♦ ♣ ♥

Whistlet

♠ ♦ ♣ ♥

This game appears to be a compact form of German Whist. Simple to play, Whistlet supplies an engaging mix of luck and skill. And you can learn to play in about one minute.

Number of players: Two.

Object: To win the most tricks.

The cards: A regular pack of 52 cards is used. Aces are high.

To play: Deal seven cards to each player, one at a time. Turn the next card over and place it face up next

to the stock. The suit of this card will be the trump suit.

Nondealer leads to the first trick. You must follow suit when you are able to; otherwise, trump or discard. A trick is won by the higher trump in it or, if it contains no trump, by the higher card of the suit led. After each trick, both players take a new card from the stock. The winner of the trick draws first and leads to the next trick.

Each deal consists of 26 tricks. The last seven tricks are played after the stock pile is gone. Winner of the 19th trick draws the remaining stock card; the loser takes the trump upcard. Keep track of individual tricks each player has won.

Scoring: The player who took the greater number of tricks scores the difference between that number and the lesser number of tricks. If both players took 13 tricks, neither scores; but if one player took 15 tricks and the other took 11, the winner scores 4 points.

Tips: Even if you are void in a suit, use judgment in trumping. It may be better strategy to shed a loser by discarding it.

In the last seven tricks, it will pay to have more trumps than your opponent.

In the illustration opposite, suppose spades are trump. With the last seven tricks to go, you should play the left hand by leading any spade in your hand until your opponent is forced to play the king. After regaining the lead, draw opponent's remaining trumps by leading a winning spade each time. Then the rest of your cards are winners, too.

♠ ♦ ♣ ♥ ♠ ♦ ♣ ♥ ♠ ♦ ♣ ♥ ♠ ♦ ♣ ♥ ♠ ♦

The trump suit contains exactly 13 cards. If you keep count of the trumps played, you'll know in the endgame just how many trumps your opponent has. As in most games, the better you remember the cards that have been played, the better you'll do. Keeping track of trumps and a few high cards is helpful, but if you can remember every card in the first part of the game, you'll know your opponent's last seven cards.

In the first phase of play, you may well discover opponent to be void of a suit. It may be a good risk to continue leading that suit, when your objective is to reduce your opponent's trumps. If your objective instead is to win your low trumps, then it may pay to lead a singleton, hoping to remain void in that suit later.

Variation: Play Whistlet just as above, but try to lose as many tricks as possible. When you must win a trick, use the highest card available. At the end of play, the one with fewer tricks scores the points.

♠ ♦ ♣ ♥

Accordion

♠ ♦ ♣ ♥

Even if you're not musical, you can while away idle moments playing the popular solitaire game Accordion. Each game is quick and requires only a small space.

Object: To form a single face-up pile of all the cards.

The cards: A regular deck of 52 cards is used.

The layout: Simply keep dealing out cards in a row.

To play: Deal cards out into a single row. When you spot matches described below, pile cards onto other cards to the left. These are the matches: (1) The two cards must be either the same suit or the same rank, and (2) the cards must be either next to each other or have two cards between.

Pile matches together onto the matched card on the left. Then treat any pile made as a single card. Look to see if one move has created another. If you have no more moves, play a new card at the end of the row.

Occasionally, a newly turned card gives two possible moves; you may make either. The game ends in a single pile very rarely; you're doing very well to get down to just two or three piles.

Dealing the ♠ 10 gives you your first move. The ♠ 10 can be piled onto its match, the ♦ 10 (same rank). The ♠ 10 now matches the ♠ 3 (same suit) two cards to the left, so the two-card pile can be moved onto the ♠ 3. Since no matches remain, continue by adding a new card to the end of the row.

Variations: Start by dealing a 13-card row, which will probably give you choices of moves to make. Before playing, you may enjoy trying to project each move's results. When you've made all your moves, add new cards to the row until 13 are again showing and proceed as before.

A similar solitaire is called Royal Wedding. Start by placing the ♥ Q on the top of the pack and the ♥ K on the bottom. Deal out the pack one card at a time, starting with the ♥ Q. As you proceed, throw out single cards and pairs of cards that stand between cards that match by suit or rank. You win the game if you wind up with just the ♥ Q and ♥ K, the Royal Marriage. It won't happen very often, but when it does, it's quite an accomplishment.

♠ ♦ ♣ ♥

Black Hole

♠ ♦ ♣ ♥

Here's a solitaire game whose name comes from those places in the universe where heavenly objects just seem to disappear!

Object: To play all the cards into the black hole—the ♠A.

The cards: A regular deck of 52 cards is used.

The layout: Place the ♠A (the Black Hole) face up in the center of the table. Make 17 piles of 3 face-up cards each around the ♠A.

To play: You can use only the top card from each pile. Play up or down in sequence onto the center (ace connects to both king and deuce). Suit does not matter. In the diagram, you can start by choosing either the ♦2, ♣2, or ♣K to play on the ♠A, and follow the chosen card with another card in sequence either up or down.

Tips: The rules are simple, but the play can wind up going in many possible directions. Try to look a few moves ahead; you may see that one line of play will lead to a dead end. Sometimes it will seem as if all options lead to a dead end. Pick one and try anyway; you might have overlooked something in your thinking.

♠ ♦ ♣ ♥

Calculation

♠ ♦ ♣ ♥

One of the older solitaire games, Calculation is a favorite of players who like a pastime requiring skill and forethought. With a little practice in waste-heap management, you can frequently win.

Object: To build on the four foundation cards in numerical sequences. Build on the ace by ones, on the 2 by twos, on the 3 by threes, and on the 4 by fours. Suit does not matter. The completed layout would look like the one on the next page.

Calculation hand.

The cards: A regular deck of 52 cards is used.

The layout: Place any A, 2, 3, and 4 in a foundation column.

To play: Turn cards up from the pack one by one, building on any foundation when possible. In the ace row, play 2, 3, 4, 5, etc. In the 2 row, play 4, 6, 8, 10, Q, etc. In the 3 row, play 3, 6, 9, Q, 2, 5, etc. Refer to the layout above for an example of how the rows are built up in a successfully completed game. Lay off unplayable cards onto one of four waste piles, as you choose. The top card of any waste pile is always available. It's customary to spread the waste heaps downward to see the cards buried within each. You may go through the pack only once.

Tips: Queens, 6s, and 8s are needed fairly early in the play, while 10s, jacks, and especially kings are needed later. Clever selection of card placement in the waste heaps is essential to succeed in this game. Some players save one waste heap for the kings.

♠ ♦ ♣ ♥ ♠ ♦ ♣ ♥ ♠ ♦ ♣ ♥ ♠ ♦ ♣ ♥ ♠ ♦

Canfield

♠ ♦ ♣ ♥

Canfield is named after the owner of a celebrated gaming house in the old-time resort town of Sarasota Springs, New York.

Object: To build four ascending suit sequences, each beginning with the foundation card. The suits are built around the corner: Ace follows king and deuce follows ace.

The cards: A regular pack of 52 cards is used.

The layout: Deal a packet of 13 cards face down. Turn the top card face up and set the packet at the left for a reserve pile. Deal another card face up above and to the right of the reserve pile. This is the first of four foundation cards. As other cards of the same rank become available, add them onto this row. Beneath this row, deal a row of four cards to start the tableau.

To play: Turn up cards from the pack in three-card bunches. The top card of a bunch is always available. If you play it, the card underneath is available. Put unused cards into a waste heap, the top card of which is available.

Add to the foundations with cards from the pack, the reserve, the tableau, or the waste heap. You may build downward sequences, alternating in color, on the tableau cards. These sequences can be built around the corner like the ascending sequences: A king can

♠ ♦ ♣ ♥ ♠ ♦ ♣ ♥ ♠ ♦ ♣ ♥ ♠ ♦ ♣ ♥ ♠ ♦

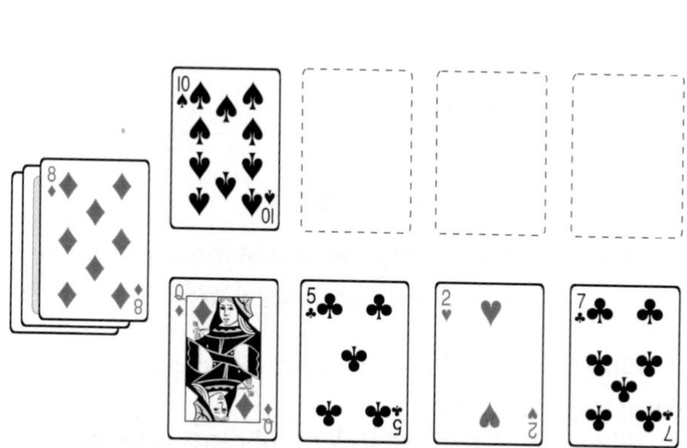

Ten is the first foundation card. There are no further moves to make in this beginning layout, so start by turning up the first bunch of three cards.

be played on an ace. You may also move an entire sequence of tableau cards onto another in order to clear a space. Spaces are filled with a card from the reserve pile. If the reserve pile is used up, fill open tableau spaces with available cards from the pack or waste heap. Turn the waste heap over each time you've gone through the pack. Keep on until the game is won or you can make no more plays.

Variation: A slight variant called Storehouse makes things a little easier for you. Always remove the four deuces in advance and use them as the foundation-row base cards. Then build on each deuce upward in suit to the ace.

♠ ♦ ♣ ♥

Cross Currents

♠ ♦ ♣ ♥

This one-deck solitaire game is also known as Corner Card and Vanishing Cross.

Object: To build up a 13-card suit sequence in each corner of the layout.

The cards: A regular deck of 52 cards is used.

The layout: The main play takes place in a grid of three by three spaces, like a Tic-Tac-Toe board. The Cross Currents spaces are the noncorner spaces in the box of nine spaces, that is, the five that form a cross shape in the middle.

To play: Start by dealing a single card face up onto each of the five Cross Currents spaces. Next, deal one card face up onto the upper left corner—this will be the base number for all four corner sequences. Turn up cards one at a time from the stock pile until this pile is depleted.

Play each card you turn face up

- **(1)** on a corner pile if it's the next higher card in that suit
- **(2)** on any Cross Currents pile, where that card is the next downward sequential card without regard to suit
- **(3)** on a Cross Currents space that may be empty
- **(4)** on the waste pile.

You may use the current top card of the waste pile for any legal play in the layout. Cards in the Cross Currents piles are also available for play (e.g., in the diagram, you can play the ♣3 onto the ♥4), but they may not go onto the waste pile, and you can move only the top card. When a Cross Currents pile becomes empty you may move one or more cards at the top of any Cross Currents pile to the empty space, move the top waste pile card to the empty space, or just turn a new card from the stock pile and place it there.

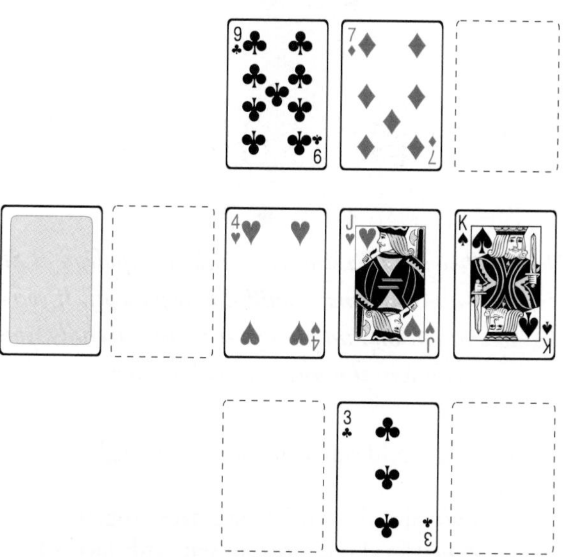

In the diagram, the ♣9 is the base card. You'll build that whole suit in upward sequence (topping ♣K with ♣A and ♣A with ♣2), ending with ♣8. When another 9 comes up, then start that suit's sequence in a new corner. Note: White areas are designated spaces without a card.

In the diagram, if the next card you turn up is the ♠9, play it in a corner location; if it's the ♣10, play it on the ♣9; if it's the ♥Q, play it below the ♠K; or if it's the ♦5, start the waste pile.

Tip: How you use the Cross Currents open spaces will influence the outcome of the play, for you have only one chance to go through the pack.

♠ ♦ ♣ ♥

Forty Thieves

♠ ♦ ♣ ♥

This challenging solitaire is also called Napoleon at St. Helena's and Big Forty. Skillful play pays off. If you pay close attention and plan your moves carefully, you can win this one reasonably often.

Object: To build suit sequences on all eight aces up to the king.

The cards: Shuffle two 52-card decks together.

The layout: Deal out a row of ten cards face up. Overlapping them slightly, deal another row of ten cards over the first row. Continue until 40 cards have been dealt in ten columns of four. Above these, leave room for eight foundations.

To play: As aces are released, place them above the layout as foundations. The bottom card of each col-

Forty Thieves

umn is available and may be played in downward suit sequence onto another available card or in upward suit sequence on a foundation pile. The tableau shown on p. 213 gives quite a few moves. You can start by stacking the ♠A, ♠2, and ♠3 on one of the foundation piles. Next, move the ♥8 on the ♥9, and then the ♥7 on the ♥8. This frees the ♣A to start another foundation pile. Note: You cannot move the ♥7 and ♥8 as a unit, but must arrange to move them one card at a time.

Turn cards up from stock one at a time. Cards that cannot be played to the tableau or foundations form a waste heap whose top card is always available. You can go through the pack once. When a column is empty, fill the space with any playable card.

Tips: Success is likely to rest with your ability to clear out one or more columns. With one or two spaces available for transportation, you can maneuver longer card sequences.

Variations: Some players allow tableau sequences to stack downward in alternating suit color. Although this does not keep the suits together, it offers twice as many possible plays and will increase your odds of winning. Another way to boost your chances is to place the eight aces into the foundation row and then deal out the "forty thieves" below.

♠ ♦ ♣ ♥

♠ ♦ ♣ ♥ ♠ ♦ ♣ ♥ ♠ ♦ ♣ ♥ ♠ ♦ ♣ ♥ ♠ ♦

Four Corners

♠ ♦ ♣ ♥

In this entertaining endeavor, each suit has its own exclusive corner. Once the layout gets started, only members may enter.

Object: To build each suit in sequence upon its corner ace.

The cards: A regular deck of 52 cards is used.

The layout: Distribute the four aces one to each corner. Deal four cards face up around each ace. In the center, leave room for the rest of the pack and a waste heap.

To play: Look for deuces anywhere in the layout to place on their appropriate aces. Look for the 3s that go on the 2s, etc. If possible, add 3s onto the 2s, and so on. (In the tableau shown on p. 216, put the ♣2 on the ♣A and the ♦2 and ♦3 on the ♦A).

Turn over cards from the pack one at a time. Discard those that can't be played into the waste heap. Refill open corner spaces with cards of the appropriate suit only. They may come from the pack, from the top of the waste pile, or from cards in the original layout.

As the game progresses, continue building up the four suit sequences whenever possible. Turn the waste heap over and go through the pack again. To win, you must complete each sequence this time.

Tips: Since you have two chances to go through the pack, it's okay to leave high cards for the second time

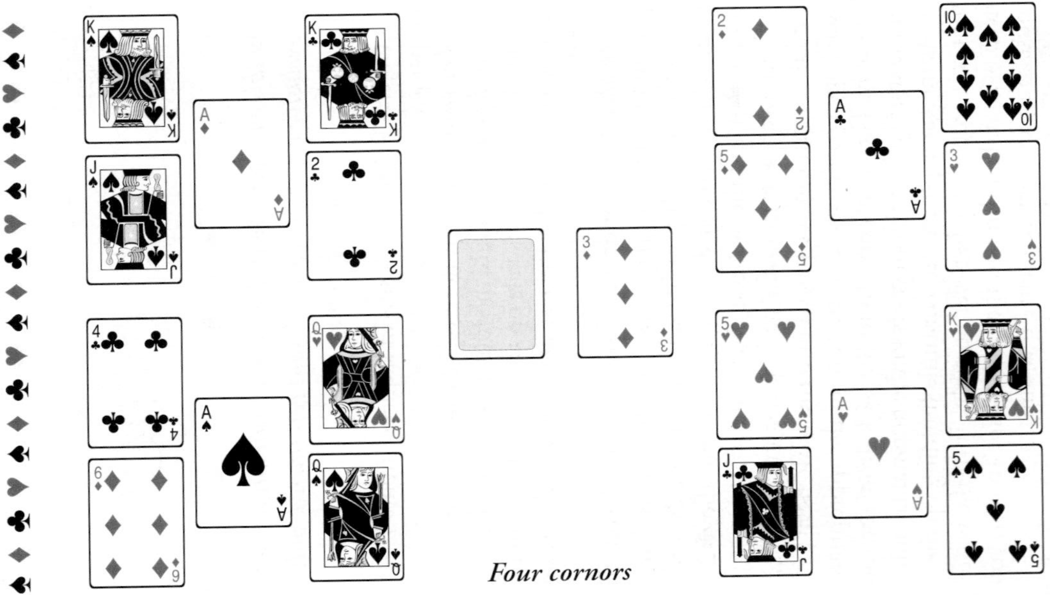

Four cornors

around. Try to "park" low cards in their correct corners, as well as any intermediate cards that might soon come into play. As spaces open up, you may have several options for filling them. Usually you should try not to fill with a high card right away, unless that opens a key low card that could get trapped in the waste heap. When several spaces are open, with no great play to make from the waste heap, it's probably better to check out the next cards from the pack. On the second time through, try not to bury any low card in the waste heap under a higher card of the same suit.

♠ ♦ ♣ ♥

Gaps

This widely known solitaire gives you a chance to put on your thinking cap. The name comes from the gaps left in the layout once play begins.

Object: To end up with four 12-card rows; each one should be a complete suit in sequence from 2 through king.

The cards: A regular deck of 52 cards is used.

The layout: Deal out the whole deck in four rows of 13 cards. Then take the four aces out of the layout and put them aside.

To play: You may fill any space with the next higher card to the card at the left of that space. For example, if a space lies to the right of the ♣10, take the ♣J from its present position and fill that space. This will leave a new space where the ♣J was.

Fill an empty space at the left end of a row with any deuce. A space behind a king cannot be filled. But if you're able to move that king behind its proper queen, the space may open up again.

When all four gaps are behind kings, card movement is blocked. Gather up all cards in the layout that aren't in their correct sequence behind deuces. Shuffle up these cards and the four aces, then deal the cards to fill out the four 13-card rows. Remove the aces as before and proceed with the play. If this layout gets stalled too, you're allowed one further redeal.

Tips: Usually three or four plays are possible at the start of a game, each opening up a series of further moves. You may see that some plays will soon lead to a useless space behind a king. To follow each line of play can be perplexing at first, but you'll get better at it after playing a few times. It helps to identify a card you would like to move and work back to see what other cards need to move before you can move that card.

Variations: A number of players handle the redeals by omitting the aces and leaving a gap in each row behind the last correctly positioned card. If a row has not yet been started, leave a gap at the left for a deuce.

♠ ♦ ♣ ♥

Good Neighbors

♠ ♦ ♣ ♥

Pay attention to this catchy little solitaire, also known as Monte Carlo or Weddings. It may look innocent enough, but some skill is required since you've got many choices in the play.

Object: To pair off and remove all the cards in the pack.

The cards: A regular deck of 52 cards is used.

The layout: Deal four rows across of five cards each, face up.

To play: Remove any pair of cards of the same rank that are vertical, diagonal, or horizontal neighbors.

Fill the spaces left by pairs taken by moving the remaining layout cards to the left, and then up and over to the end of the row above. Fill in the spaces that remain at the end of the layout with new cards from the pack. Then start looking for more "good neighbors."

Continue removing pairs until the whole pack is taken. If at any turn the layout has no matches, the game is lost.

Tip: When dealing with a choice of plays, consider the various outcomes.

♠ ♦ ♣ ♥

♠ ♦ ♣ ♥ ♠ ♦ ♣ ♥ ♠ ♦ ♣ ♥ ♠ ♦ ♣ ♥ ♠ ♦

Grandfather's Clock

♠ ♦ ♣ ♥

This rousing solitaire is sure to keep you ticking. Play your cards right and bide your time—and you'll wind up with a picture-perfect finish.

Object: To build upward suit sequences on each foundation card, aces following kings. When the game is won, all cards have been played out and an ace sits at one o'clock, a deuce is at two o'clock, a trey at three o'clock, and so on, with a jack at 11 o'clock and a queen at 12 o'clock.

The cards: Two decks of 52 cards.

The layout: From a double deck, select 2, 6, 10 of one suit, 3, 7, J of another, 4, 8, Q of a third suit, and 5, 9, K of the fourth suit. Arrange them in numerical order as in the face of a clock, with the 6 placed at one o'clock. These 12 cards are the foundations.

Next deal three circles of 12 cards each face up and overlapping around the outside of the clock face, as shown. These are reserves. The remaining cards form the stock.

To play: Turn cards from the stock one by one, going through the pack just one time. Discards go into a single waste heap whose top card is always

Here's a typical Grandfather's Clock layout.

available. On the tableau, only the outermost reserve cards are available. A card played will release the one beneath it.

You may build onto the foundation piles from the reserves, the stock, or the waste heap. Play onto available reserve cards in downward suit sequence. You may move as a single unit a group of cards that are all connected in downward suit sequence.

When any reserve pile has fewer than three cards, fill its available slots only from the unseen stock and never from the waste heap or from other reserves.

Tips: You can win Grandfather's Clock fairly often if you make the most sensible plays and watch what's going on. Often you'll have quite a few plays and sometimes even a choice of plays between identical cards. Look to see which cards would be released by each alternative.

♠ ♦ ♣ ♥

Klondike

♠ ♦ ♣ ♥

For many people klondike is synonymous with solitaire. Why it has been so popular is a puzzle, since you don't end up a winner very often.

Object: To release the four aces and build sequences in suit on them.

The cards: A regular deck of 52 cards is used.

The layout: Deal a row of seven cards with the leftmost one face up and the rest face down. On top of the face-down cards, deal another row of cards, with the leftmost of these face up. Keep doing this until you have seven piles, ranging from one card on the left to seven cards on the right, with the top cards face up. The remainder of the cards form the stock.

To play: As aces become available, they go into a foundation row above the layout. You can build downward sequences on the cards in the layout in

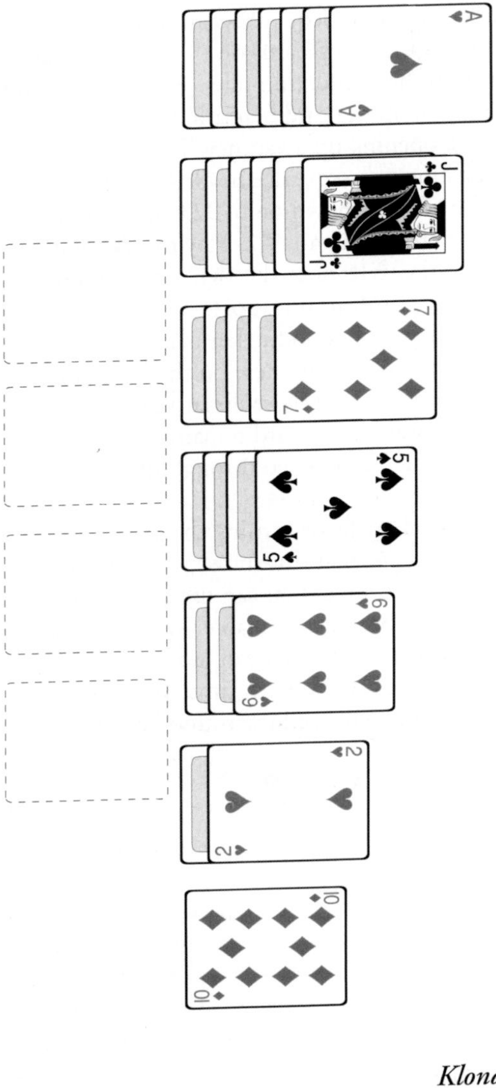

Klondike

alternating color only. Sequences can be moved to other piles as a unit. Top cards on the piles are available to put on the foundation piles. As cards move off their piles, turn up the card beneath. Occasionally a pile empties, opening up a vacancy. This can be filled only with a king or a sequence headed by a king.

With the tableau shown on p. 223, start a foundation pile with the ♥A and ♥2. Play the ♠5 onto the ♥6, and the ♦10 onto the ♣J. This will give you several new cards to turn up!

When the layout has no further plays, turn cards singly from the stock. Play these on the foundations or layout if possible; otherwise discard into a waste heap. The top waste-heap card remains available until another covers it. You may go through the stock only once.

Variations: Many favor turning the stock in bunches of three. At first this shows you only every third card, but as soon as you can use a card, then the one below it also becomes available. When the pack runs out, just turn the waste heap over and go through it in threes again. Each time, you'll see new cards unless none were used the round before.

♠ ♦ ♣ ♥ ♠ ♦ ♣ ♥ ♠ ♦ ♣ ♥ ♠ ♦ ♣ ♥ ♠ ♦

Lucky Fours

♠ ♦ ♣ ♥

This is a "lucky" solitaire because you have a very good chance to win, yet you appear to be making one sensational play after another. For this reason, have several onlookers around.

Object: To release the four aces and build complete sequences in suit up to the king.

The cards: A regular deck of 52 cards is used.

The layout: Deal 13 four-card fans face up on the table, so that all cards are visible.

To play: The top card or card sequence in any fan may be moved to the top of another group, in descending order and alternate colors. In the illustration shown on p. 226, move the ♠A and ♣A to a row above the fans to begin the suit foundations. Move the ♣4 to the ♦5, releasing the ♦3, which can be placed on the ♣4. Now you can move the ♥A.

When a space opens up, use any available king or sequence headed by a king to fill the space. Continue in this manner, freeing up new cards, or play off onto the foundations until all four of the aces have been built to kings or until the game is blocked and you can't go on.

Tips: Keep making sequences at the ends of fans. This will help you to unload them later on their foundations. When you have a choice of similar plays to make, such as two red eights to go on a black 9,

♠ ♦ ♣ ♥ ♠ ♦ ♣ ♥ ♠ ♦ ♣ ♥ ♠ ♦ ♣ ♥ ♠ ♦

look ahead to what the result of either play may bring and choose accordingly.

♠ ♦ ♣ ♥

♠ ♦ ♣ ♥ ♠ ♦ ♣ ♥ ♠ ♦ ♣ ♥ ♠ ♦ ♣ ♥ ♠ ♦

Miss Mulligan

♠ ♦ ♣ ♥

Whoever she was, Miss Milligan has given her name to one of the most popular of the double-deck solitaire games. It's similar to Spider in that successive deals cover up the work you've done.

Object: To build suit sequences on the eight aces.

The cards: Shuffle two 52-card decks together.

The layout: Deal out a row of eight cards face up.

To play: First move up any aces to the foundation row. The eight cards can be played onto each other in downward sequences of alternating colors. A sequence can be moved as a unit. Vacancies can be filled only by a king or a sequence headed by a king. When you've made all the moves you can, deal another eight cards face up overlapping the first row of cards, filling in any holes in the layout. See illustration p. 228.

After you have dealt all the cards, a unique feature called weaving comes into play. You have the option of removing one card or sequence from the layout and setting it aside in order to play the card underneath it. If later you are able to build this card or sequence back onto the layout or onto the foundation, you can set aside another card or sequence.

♠ ♦ ♣ ♥

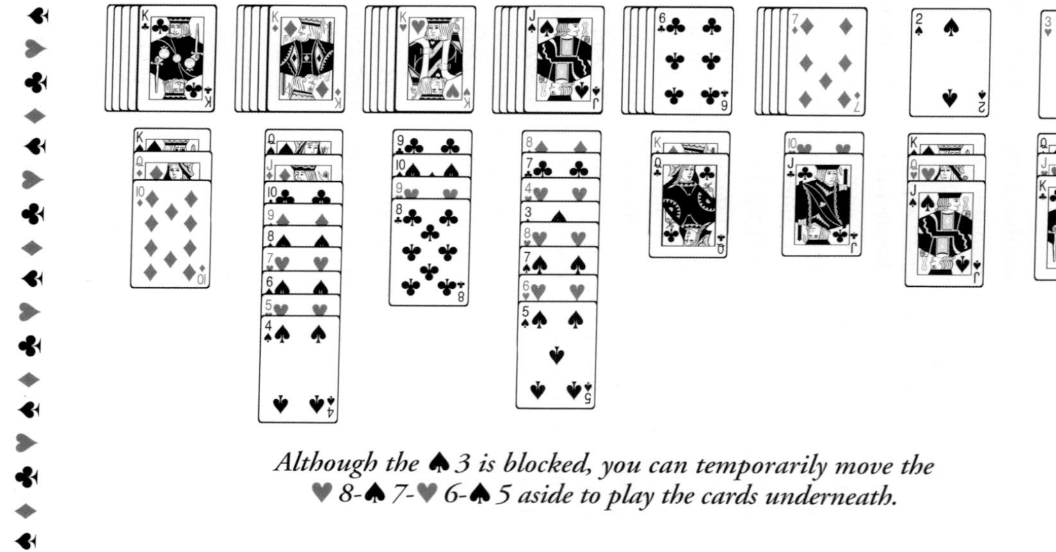

Although the ♠3 is blocked, you can temporarily move the ♥8-♠7-♥6-♠5 aside to play the cards underneath.

♠ ♦ ♣ ♥ ♠ ♦ ♣ ♥ ♠ ♦ ♣ ♥ ♠ ♦ ♣ ♥ ♠ ♦

Osmosis

♠ ♦ ♣ ♥

It's not clear how this popular, luck-driven solitaire game got such a scientific name. You'll win at this game only a bit more often than you find buried treasure.

Object: To build a chain of 13 cards in each suit. These suit chains need not be in order.

The cards: A regular deck of 52 cards is used.

The layout: Deal, face down, a column of four packets of four cards each. Turn up the top card on each. Deal the next card face up and to the right of the top packet. This card, and the three others of the same rank will be—as they show up—the four foundation bases. The remaining cards form the stock.

To play: Across the first row, play any cards from the tableau of the same suit as the foundation card. Overlap them enough so that all cards are seen. As the top card is played from each of the piles at left, turn over the next card. The piles are not refilled when they are depleted.

Turn up cards from the pack in three-card bunches. The top card of a bunch is always available. If you play it, the card underneath is available. Unused cards go into a waste heap.

As soon as the next base-number card appears, use it to begin a second suit chain in a row underneath the first. You can now add on any card of this second

You can play ♦ 8 on the ♦ row, since ♠ 8 is already in the row above. But you can't play ♣J since ♦J has not yet appeared in the row just above.

suit, but only if the card of the same rank is already in the row above.

Each new row must start off with the card of the correct base number. You can join a new card to a suit chain as long as the card of the same rank already appears in the suit chain just above.

Turn the waste heap over each time you've gone through the pack. Play on until the game is won or (more likely) blocked.

Variation: Since a blockage in any tableau pile will doom the game, some players follow the variant called Peek. The four piles are dealt face up to show their contents. This permits you to see a hopeless blockage and lets you abandon the deal.

♠ ♦ ♣ ♥

Poker Solitaire

♠ ♦ ♣ ♥

Poker Solitaire lets you play up to 12 Poker hands at once, and you can keep score to see how well you're doing. It can also be played by two.

Object: To arrange the 25 cards into high-scoring five-card poker combinations.

The cards: A regular deck of 52 cards is used.

The layout: Place 25 cards one by one face up into a grid of five columns and five rows.

Poker Solitaire Scoring:

See "Poker," page 138 for definitions of the Poker hands.

Royal flush	100
Straight flush	75
Four of a kind	50
Full house	25
Flush	20
Straight	15
Three of a kind	10
Two pair	5
One pair	2

To play: Shuffle the pack and turn up cards one at a time. Place each card within the framework of an imaginary five-by-five grid of cards. You may place each card wherever you wish in the grid, and once you place a card you can't move it. After you've played 25 cards, it's time to tally your score for the game. Total up the scores for 12 Poker hands: the five columns, the five rows, and the two diagonals. A good score is 200.

The scoring table above is the American version, which considers the likelihood of getting each hand in actual Poker.

Tips: You'll increase your chances of making straights if you avoid putting an ace, 2, queen, or king in the center of the grid. Don't plan on lots of straight flushes, but leave some chances open early in the play.

Just don't wait too long to convert three cards or even four cards held for a straight flush when it's possible to make a straight hand or a flush hand.

Variations: Some players do not count the two diagonal hands to make it further difficult. To play the two-player version, one player deals out the 25 cards face up, but not into a five-by-five grid, and the other player pulls out the same cards from a separate deck. Each player then makes their own grid with their respective cards in sight of each other if they wish.

♠ ♦ ♣ ♥

Propeller

♠ ♦ ♣ ♥

Also called The Windmill, this attractive solitaire can be won often with attentive play. The name comes from the Propeller's "wings," which appear to spin around on the tableau.

Object: To build four successive ace-to-king sequences in a single pile upon the center ace and one downward king-to-ace sequence on each of the four king foundations. The sequences are built without regard to suit.

The cards: Shuffle two 52-card decks together.

The layout: Take any ace from the pack and place

it in the center of the layout. Place two cards face up in a column above the ace and two face up below it. Place two cards in a row to the ace's left and two to the ace's right. These eight cards are the wings. The first four kings, as they turn up, go in the four positions diagonal to the ace.

To play: Deal the cards from the pack one by one;

either play them on one of the five foundations or discard them into a single waste pile. The top card of the waste pile can be played onto a foundation. The cards in the wings are also available to be played. Refill spaces in the wings with cards from either the waste pile or the stock.

You're allowed to remove a card from a king-to-ace foundation to put on the center foundation, but only one at a time. Your next play to the center has to be from the pack, the wings, or the waste pile.

Keep going until both packs play out onto the foundations or until the pack has been dealt out and the game is blocked. No redeal is allowed in this game.

♠ ♦ ♣ ♥

Seventeens

♠ ♦ ♣ ♥

Here's a simple-looking solitaire that actually has many options in the play. An experienced player can win as often as not!

Object: To discard pairs of cards that total 17 or any A-2-3 sequences (suit does not matter) from the layout until the deck is entirely depleted.

The cards: A regular deck of 52 cards is used.

The layout: Deal out ten face-up piles of three

Place the piles conveniently before you.

cards each. In the center of the table, deal a row of three upcards from the stock pile.

To play: Simply remove any pairs that add up to 17 and A-2-3 sequences, using only the top card of the ten piles and any of the three upcards. (A=1, K=13, Q=12, J=11.) In the layout shown, you could remove the ♣9 and the ♥8, the ♣4 and either the ♠K or ♦K, the ♠A-♣2-♥3, and so on. Replace center upcards only with new cards from stock; do not use any cards from the other piles to fill these spaces. You win if you can discard all 52 cards according to the rules.

Tip: You'll usually have a choice of plays to make. In general, because you must play out the entire deck, including the cards left in the stock pile, you should work on removing and replacing the three center cards. You'll have your best chance at this by keeping the other cards out in the open as long as possible.

♠ ♦ ♣ ♥

The Snake

♠ ♦ ♣ ♥

This unusual solitaire is suspenseful to play and leaves a pleasing picture. Although it's very easy to win this game, you'll find it an absorbing pastime.

Object: To build eight-card sequences on each of the 13 foundation cards in the tableau. When successful, both packs will be played out, with the cards showing in value from the ace through the king.

The cards: Shuffle two 52-card packs together.

The layout: Arrange 13 sequential cards of any suit, beginning with a 7, into a Z-shaped tableau.

To play: Deal cards up one by one and play in upward sequence on foundations whenever possible. Suit does not matter in this game. Cards turned that cannot be played are deposited in either of two waste heaps. The top card of each waste heap remains available for play and reveals the card beneath if

This is the Z-shaped starting layout for The Snake. Seven cards played in order on the 7, making a pile of eight, will have a top card of ace.

played. No moves from one waste heap to another are permitted.

Tips: Skill in placing cards onto the two waste piles is what really makes a difference. For example, an 8 that is placed on a 9 in the waste pile is usually a good play, because if the 8 plays later, so can the 9. You should try to avoid placing cards in ascending order for this reason. However, since there are many playoff piles, such a play might not be fatal.

♠ ♦ ♣ ♥

Spider

♠ ♦ ♣ ♥

This tough solitaire appeals to those who seek a formidable challenge. To conquer it, good judgment must combine with better luck. It was Franklin D. Roosevelt's favorite solitaire.

Object: To form, within the layout, eight suit sequences in downward order from king to ace. Sequences thus formed are taken out of the layout.

The cards: Shuffle together two 52-card packs.

The layout: Deal a row of ten cards face down. Deal three more rows of ten cards face down on top of the first row. Deal an additional card to each of the first four piles. Then lay a card face up on each of the ten piles. Hold the remaining 50 cards aside as a stock.

To play: All the action is within the tableau. You may play an upcard onto any card one rank above it, regardless of suit. You can move as a unit a sequence of cards in the same suit. Otherwise cards move singly. No card can be played onto an ace. A king or sequence headed by a king can move only into an empty space.

Whenever a face-down card is uncovered, turn it up. When a pile empties, fill its space with any available card or natural sequence.

When you run out of moves or choose to make no new ones, deal another row of ten cards face up onto the layout. First you must fill in any spaces in the

Spider

layout. When the whole new row is in place, you can continue playing.

Whenever you produce an entire suit sequence, you may remove it from play immediately. Or you may keep it in play if breaking it up can keep the game alive.

Tips: On the original deal, you want to get as many face-down cards uncovered as you can. Move cards onto cards of the same suit if possible. If such a move is not available, move top-ranking cards first. In the example shown opposite, move the ♦6 onto the ♦7 first. You might turn up a useful card under the ♦6. If not, move the ♣Q onto the ♦K, and either ♠9 onto the ♥10. Each new row of ten cards is a mixed blessing—you get ten new cards to deal with, but they block all the work you've done on the layout so far.

♠ ♦ ♣ ♥ ♠ ♦ ♣ ♥ ♠ ♦ ♣ ♥ ♠ ♦ ♣ ♥ ♠ ♦

The Sultan of Turkey

♠ ♦ ♣ ♥

The most delightful feature of this solitaire is the pattern it creates when you win. You'll be treated to a view of the Sultan—the king of hearts—surrounded by his harem of eight queens.

Object: To build suit sequences from ace to queen on the seven outside kings and from deuce to queen on the ace. The central king of hearts is not built on.

The cards: Two 52-card decks.

The layout: From a double deck, remove the eight kings and one ace. Arrange them in three rows of three, with a king of hearts in the center and the ace beneath it. The cards surrounding the king of hearts are the foundations. Add a column of four cards face up on each side of this array. These cards are available to play on the foundations. The remaining cards form the stock.

To play: Deal cards from the stock one by one, playing them either on the foundations or to a single waste pile. The top card of the waste pile is available for play, as are the cards from the two side columns, onto the foundations. Vacancies in the columns are

♠ ♦ ♣ ♥ ♠ ♦ ♣ ♥ ♠ ♦ ♣ ♥ ♠ ♦ ♣ ♥ ♠ ♦

A sample setup of The Sultan of Turkey.

filled from the waste pile or the stock. You are allowed two redeals, which is usually enough to make the game come out.

♠ ♦ ♣ ♥

♠ ♦ ♣ ♥ ♠ ♦ ♣ ♥ ♠ ♦ ♣ ♥ ♠ ♦ ♣ ♥ ♠ ♦

Tut's Tomb

♠ ♦ ♣ ♥

This is a version of a widely popular solitaire called Pyramid. Here the king of spades represents King Tutankhamen and rests atop a pyramid of cards.

Object: To play off all the cards in pairs that add up to 13. Aces count 1, jacks 11, and queens 12. Kings count 13 and are removed alone.

The cards: A regular deck of 52 cards is used.

The layout: Put the ♠K down first and create a pyramid of overlapping rows as shown. The last row will have seven cards. Keep the rest of the pack as a stock.

To play: Remove all pairs of available cards in the layout that total 13. Only cards not overlapped by other cards are available.

In the layout shown opposite, remove the ♣10 and the ♦3. Now the ♣8 and the ♦5 can be removed as a pair, since picking up the 8 frees the 5.

Turn cards from the stock, one at a time, to look for matches with available cards in the pyramid. Start a waste heap with cards that cannot be used with the top card of the waste heap available to play. To win, all the cards in the pyramid and in the stock pile have to be paired off. You can go through the stock pile only once.

♠ ♦ ♣ ♥

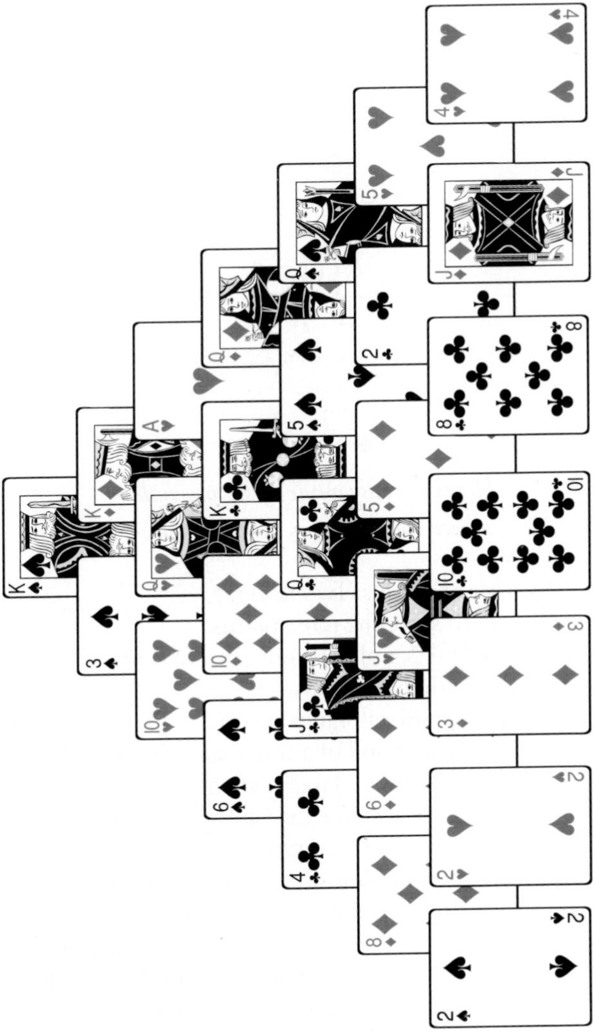

♠ ♦ ♣ ♥ ♠ ♦ ♣ ♥ ♠ ♦ ♣ ♥ ♠ ♦ ♣ ♥ ♠ ♦

Bonus Game

Dave Galt's Game of Queens

♠ ♦ ♣ ♥

Here's an easy game of sly psychology, where everyone has a chance to win!

Number of players: Two to eight.

Object: To score the most points.

The cards: If 2-4 players, one pack of cards. If more, two packs, with different backs.

To play: Remove all kings and jacks. Then give each player an 11-card hand of a single suit: Q (high) 10 9 8 7 6 5 4 3 2 A (low). Players pick up their cards.

Each player selects one card and places it on the table face down. When everyone has selected a card, turn them up to see whose is highest. If one player has the lone highest card, that player wins all the cards. But if more than one player has the highest card, each wins back only that card, and the remaining cards go to whoever has the next highest card.

When these cards have been taken in, players again select one card from those remaining in their hand, for the next showdown.

Scoring: After all 11 rounds, players count up their points. Q's tally 12, while all other cards count their face value (Ace counts 1). Record each player's score. You can either play a fixed number of deals, or play to a point total such as 200 or 500.

Everyone keeps their original suits, to make it easy to sort cards out for the next hand.

In this play, the player who had the ♣9 wins all the cards.

Here, the ♣ Q and ♥ Q cancel each other out, and the player of the ♦ 7 wins the rest of the cards.

Tip: Everyone is guaranteed at least 12 points for their Queen, but you want to play your Queen when no one else does. It's clear that the longer players hold on to their Queens, the more likely they will play them at the same time. Should you play it early? Not if someone else thinks so at the same moment you do. This is where the cagey thinking begins.

Variation: All players select their 11-card order ahead of time, leave the cards in a face-down pile. For

Here, the ♣Q and ♥ Q cancel each other out, but so do the ♦ 7 and ♠ 7, and so in this rare instance, each player wins back the card they played!

each round, every one simply turns over the top card on their stack. While the pace is quicker, there's less play-by-play strategy.

♠ ♦ ♣ ♥

Glossary

♠ ♦ ♣ ♥

Bella: In Klaberjass, the king and queen of trumps.

Bid: A spoken declaration to win a specified number of tricks or points; also, to make such a declaration.

Big Casino: In Casino, the ten of diamonds.

Blucher: In Nap, one of three bids to take five tricks.

Build: In Casino, to combine two or more cards so they can be taken with another card; also, the combination itself.

Canasta: In Canasta, a natural canasta is a meld of seven cards of the same rank. In a mixed canasta, from one to three cards are replaced by wild cards.

Contract: An agreement to win a certain number of tricks or points in a game or round.

Crib: In Cribbage, the extra hand, belonging to the dealer, formed by the players' discards.

Cutthroat: Each player playing on his or her own.

Deadwood: In Gin Rummy, unmatched cards in a hand.

Deal: The act of portioning out the cards to the players; also, the period of play in the game between one deal and the next.

Declaration: A statement to fulfill a contract.

Deuce: A card of the rank of two; also called a two-spot.

Dix: In Pinochle, the lowest trump.

Draw trumps: To lead high trumps in order to deplete opponent's hand of trumps.

Draw: To take a new card or cards.

Face card: A king, queen, or jack.

Face value: The numerical value of a card.

Flush: A set of cards all of the same suit.

Follow suit: To play a card of the suit led.

Foundation: In solitaire, a starting card on which other specific cards are played.

Full house: In Poker, a hand with three of a kind and a pair.

Game: A total number of points to achieve; also, what constitutes winning or ending a game.

Gin: In Gin Rummy, a hand completely matched in melding sets, with no deadwood.

Going out: Playing, melding, or discarding your final card.

Hand: The cards dealt to a player; also, the period of play in the game between one deal and the next.

Jass: In Klaberjass, the jack of trump.

Kitty: A common chip pool; also (in a few games) cards available for exchange.

Knock: In Rummy and Gin Rummy, to end play by laying down a hand that is not completely matched.

Lay off: To play one or more cards according to allowable plays.

Lead: To play the first card to a trick.

Left bower: In Euchre, the jack of the same color as the trump suit.

Little Casino: In Casino, the two of spades.

Maker: A player who takes on a specific obligation, such as to take a certain number of points or tricks, often along with the right to choose the trump suit.

Marriage: A meld consisting of the king and queen.

Match: To equate by being of the same rank (or by another criterion).

Meld: A combination of cards with scoring value, generally three or more cards in sequence in one suit or all of the same rank; also, to show or play such a combination.

Menel: In Klaberjass, the 9 of trump.

Misère: In Nap, a bid of three no trump.

Napoleon: In Nap, one of three bids to take five tricks.

No-trump: The condition when no suit is trumps in a trick-taking game.

Pass: A spoken declaration not to make a bid; in Hearts, three hidden cards exchanged among the players.

Peg: In Cribbage, to score points.

Plain card: Any 10, 9, 8, 7, 6, 5, 4, 3, 2, or ace.

Pot: A pile of chips or counters to be collected by the winner.

Quartet: In Cribbage, four cards of the same rank.

Reserve: In solitaire, a group of cards available to be played.

Right bower: In Euchre, the jack of the trump suit.

Royal flush: In Poker, an ace-high straight flush.

Schmeiss: In Klaberjass, a proposal to either accept the upcard as trump or throw in the deal.

Sequence: Two or more cards in consecutive order.

Singleton: A holding of only one card in a suit.

Speculation: In 2-10-Jack, the ace of spades, which is the highest-ranking card.

Stock: The undealt cards available for future use.

Straight: In Poker, five cards in sequence but not in the same suit.

Straight flush: In Poker, five cards in sequence and in the same suit.

Table: The playing area; also, to lay down a meld on the playing area.

Tableau: In solitaire, the layout of cards on the playing surface, not including the foundations.

Talon: A portion of the pack reserved for later use during the deal.

Trail: In Casino, to play a card without building on or taking in other cards.

Trey: A card of the rank of three, also called a three-spot.

Trick: A round of cards played, one from each player's hand.

Triplet: In Cribbage, three cards of the same rank.

Trump: A suit designated to be higher ranking than any other suit; any card in that suit. Also, to play a trump card on a trick.

Undercut: In Gin Rummy, to show a hand with deadwood counting less than or equal to the knocker's hand.

Upcard: The first card turned up after a deal, often to begin play or initiate a discard pile.

Void: A lack of a suit in a player's hand.

Wellington: In Nap, one of three bids to take five tricks.

Wild card: A card or cards, established before the game begins, that can be designated by the holder to stand for any other card.